Handbook on Artificial Intelligence and Expert Systems in Law Enforcement

HANDBOOK ON ARTIFICIAL INTELLIGENCE AND EXPERT SYSTEMS IN LAW ENFORCEMENT

Edward C. Ratledge
and
Joan E. Jacoby

Foreword by Cornelius J. Behan

GREENWOOD PRESS
New York • Westport, Connecticut • London

Library of Congress Cataloging-in-Publication Data

Ratledge, Edward C.
   Handbook on artificial intelligence and expert systems in law
enforcement / Edward C. Ratledge and Joan E. Jacoby ;   foreword by Cornelius Behan.
      p. cm.
   Bibliography: p.
   Includes index.
   ISBN 0-313-26461-9 (lib. bdg. : alk. paper)
   1. Information storage and retrieval systems—Law enforcement.
   2. Police—United States—Data Processing—Case studies.
   3. Artificial intelligence.   4. Expert systems (Computer science)
   I. Jacoby, Joan E.   II. Title.
   HV7936.A8R38   1989
   363.2'3'0285633—dc20   89-7467

British Library Cataloguing in Publication Data is available.

Library of Congress Catalog Card Number: 89-7467
ISBN: 0-313-26461-9

First published in 1989

Greenwood Press, Inc.
88 Post Road West, Westport, Connecticut 06881

Printed in the United States of America

The paper used in this book complies with the
Permanent Paper Standard issued by the National
Information Standards Organization (Z39.48-1984).

10 9 8 7 6 5 4 3 2 1

To all those who would rather be criticized
for trying something that might fail
than be critized for doing nothing at all.

CONTENTS

Figures   ix

Foreword   xi

Preface and Acknowledgments   xiii

Introduction   xvii

1. Expert Systems for Law Enforcement   1

2. Expert Systems and Policing Issues   15

3. Applications in Expert Systems   39

4. Building an Expert System   57

5. Some Fundamentals of Artificial Intelligence   81

6. Data Processing and the Expert System   99

7. Case Study of the Baltimore County Police
Department's Expert System   117

Appendix A: Technical Terms and Glossary   131

Appendix B: Expert System Vendors and
AI Publications   141

Appendix C: Selected Bibliography on Policing   155

Appendix D: Selected Technical Bibliography   173

References   183

Index   191

FIGURES

4.1	Framework for Residential Burglaries	64
4.2	Components of Computer-Aided Dispatch	66
4.3	Components of Career Criminal/Repeat Offender	67
4.4	Selected Rules by Type and Probability	71
5.1	Reasoning Methods - Forward Reasoning	89
5.2	Reasoning Methods - Backward Reasoning	89
5.3	Search Strategies - Breadth First	90
5.4	Search Strategies - Depth First	90
5.5	Comparison of TRUE/FALSE Combinations with IMPLY Operator	94

FOREWORD

Today's typical law enforcement agency is challenged by the daily necessity of meeting the expanding needs of the public with only limited resources. Police departments everywhere are confronted by escalating street and gun-related violence, and other traditional and non-traditional demands for service, while coping at the same time with constantly changing priorities, uncertain or shrinking resources, and fewer seasoned personnel. These stresses can lead police executives to adopt a defensive or "siege" mentality, where protecting the status quo becomes acceptable, and is more comfortable than exploring new avenues that might lead to a more efficient and productive use of resources. In fact, these trying times are precisely the occasion when senior police officials should seize the initiative and search for and experiment with new techniques and technologies.

Perhaps the best example of the reluctance of law enforcement to change the status quo has involved automated data processing, brought about by the introduction of the computer into twentieth century life. The private sector began adapting to this change as early as the 1960s; only in the 1980s can law enforcement claim a similar, comprehensive adaptation. Lest one misinterprets, I hasten to add that while police take risks every day, those are "on the street" risks for which we have trained and prepared. Now that the fear of the computer has been faced and mastered, law enforcement in the 1990s must show leadership and foresight in planning for and adopting the next generation of automation--computer assisted investigation and decision-making.

The *Handbook on Artificial Intelligence and Expert Systems in Law Enforcement* is a guide which attempts to demystify the use of the methods   of artificial intelligence by police agencies. Such state-of-the-art methods have been instituted to date by only a handful of police departments around the world.   Yet, expert systems are clearly applicable to policing.   Current applications have demonstrated that seasoned detectives can have an "expert assistant" to relieve them of the routine aspects of investigation; rookie police officers can have an "expert instructor" to lead them through unfamiliar tasks; and dispatchers can have an "expert consultant" to guide them through various assignment strategies.   The potential of expert systems is probably limited only by the imagination of those leading and managing our police forces.

A police administrator who utilizes an expert system can revitalize personnel who are challenged by working smarter, not harder.

The technology is ready. Are you?

Cornelius J. Behan

Chief of Police
Baltimore County Police Department

PREFACE AND ACKNOWLEDGMENTS

The application of expert systems in the law enforcement environment is relatively new. As a result, there is little literature that specifically discusses its potential value or impact on police operations and management. Yet the need for information is important given the growing use of expert systems to improve decision-making under emergency conditions. Law enforcement applications include computer-aided dispatching and emergency medical services; assisting the solution of high-volume crimes, such as residential burglaries; aiding in the design of programs for the apprehension and prosecution of career criminals and repeat offenders; and upgrading personnel through better training programs. Colleges and universities also have limited materials about the application of expert systems and other aspects of artificial intelligence in criminal justice. The effect is twofold. Criminal justice departments recognize the need for reference books and computer science departments need materials that provide real-world applications for their students. Therefore, this book has been written for both practitioners and the academic community.

This book provides law enforcement officials with information about how expert systems can be applied to law enforcement activities. It discusses the impact of these systems on traditional ways of policing and crime-solving. It presents practical guidelines for jurisdictions considering the implementation of expert systems. It is also designed to supplement college and university research and teaching materials for computer science and criminal justice curricula.

All books have their roots in some earlier time and are as much the result of the innovations and imaginations of others as they are of the authors. The roots for this book can be found in England, specifically in the Devon and Cornwall Constabulary, headquartered in Exeter. Sparked by the imagination and foresight of J. Brian Morgan, deputy chief constable, and in collaboration with John Hulburt, chief superintendent and David W. B. Webb, superintendent, the force embarked upon a crime program so comprehensive that it had no imitators in either England or the United States. The support of Messrs. Morgan, Hulburt, and Webb for our work in the United States cannot be undervalued or overpraised.

We were fortunate to find their professional counterpart in a courageous chief of police, Cornelius Behan, who was willing to experiment with this new technology, provide support, and to bring the professional stature to the Baltimore County, Maryland, Police Department to the project. His dedication was complemented by the expertise and experience of his assistant, Kai Martensen. With over twenty years of multi-faceted criminal justice experience, Kai not only was instrumental in the development of the expert system for the Baltimore County Police Department, but also acted as an expert in developing the career criminal/repeat offender expert system. His knowledge, advice, and experience had a substantial influence on this book.

As with most other innovative projects in criminal justice, federal involvement, support, and assistance are invaluable. Grants were provided by the National Institute of Justice for developing the proto-type expert system for residential burglaries and the Bureau of Justice Assistance for supporting demonstration projects in this area and that of career criminals and repeat offender programs. Our gratitude is extended to James K. (Chips) Stewart, director of the National Institute of Justice, and Dr. Edwin Zedlewski, senior staff economist. The extension of this work into other areas of expert systems could not have been possible without the support of the Bureau of Justice Assistance, its directors, George A. Luciano, and his successor, Charles Smith, and James Swain, director of Discretionary Grants. As our project monitor and advisor, Fred L. Becker is our strongest supporter in the agency.

We are grateful for the support and opportunity provided by Provost L. Leon Campbell of the University of Delaware, Dean David Ames, and our colleagues at the College of Urban Affairs and Public Policy. The professional environment of this institution and that of the Jefferson Institute for Justice Studies helped the conceptual development of this book and facilitated its writing.

For lending expertise to bridging the gap between conventional data processing and the world of artificial intelligence, we are indebted to John Falcone and the gang at University Computing Services Corporation.

We thank Ron Allen, research analyst at the Jefferson Institute, who procured and processed many of the materials for this book. His unfailing good humor in the midst of the most tedious work helped move this book to completion in a timely fashion.

Finally, we gratefully acknowledge Pauline DelMauro of the Jefferson Institute, who edited, formatted, and re-edited the materials and who had the painstaking job of compiling all the materials into book form and placing it in final form.

To all the others unnamed but not unknown to us, we thank you for your help, patience, and, most importantly, your generosity of spirit and cooperation.

INTRODUCTION

The task of combining technical detail with operational program information is difficult; but it is even more complicated when the audience includes diverse groups such as police chiefs, computer systems specialists, and criminal justice students. Clearly the policy issues that concern the chief of police are of limited interest to the computer programming staff, and the management and operational procedures that must be dev_loped by captains and sergeants are only of passing interest to the executive office. Adding substantive information about policing to the applications described in this book for students in a higher educational environment makes the task even more complex.

To minimize the confusion that could result with improperly presented materials, we adopted the following strategy for presenting the materials in this book. We assembled the information in an order that moves from a general discussion of the subject matter to a description of technical aspects important to the adoption of expert systems applications. Chapters 1 and 2 provide an overview of expert systems as they apply to different law enforcement activities and discuss the policy implications of those operations. Chapter 3 describes practical applications for expert systems in computer-aided dispatching, crime-solving, and training. From these descriptions, practitioners should be able to gauge the impact that expert systems might have on their commands, operations, and administration. Chapter 4 introduces the reader to expert systems. It is directed to those interested in the actual development of these systems in the context of law enforcement. This chapter outlines the basic components of expert systems, and discusses their characteristics and terminology. It introduces the layperson to the subject and assumes little prior knowledge of computers or automated systems. Chapter 5 provides a basic introduction to the field of artificial intelligence. This presentation should be of interest to technical personnel who have a knowledge of data processing but not of AI. It should also find an audience in anyone who is interested in learning how artificial intelligence is used in problem solving and, in particular, expert systems. Chapter 6 is written for the potential expert systems designer or the manager of the data-processing division. It discusses the problems encountered in linking inferencing to data processing and the efficiencies and technical requirements of the system. Finally, Chapter 7 contains a case study of the Baltimore County Police Department's expert system for residential burglaries. It describes chronologically the steps taken in the development of the system and discusses costs and impact.

The end materials contain a list of vendors in expert systems, a glossary, and two bibliographies. One bibliography surveys the recent literature relating to current police issues and is annotated, the other lists references to publications relating to expert systems and automation in the law enforcement area.

Handbook on Artificial Intelligence and Expert Systems in Law Enforcement

1
EXPERT SYSTEMS FOR LAW ENFORCEMENT

The headlines read " 'Big Floyd' All Wired Up to Aid G-Men" (*Washington Post*, 20 July 1986); "Detectives on Disks: Law Enforcers Use New Computer Software to Solve Crimes" (*Wall Street Journal*, 11 September 1987). The stories they tell are about the use of artificial intelligence and expert systems in dealing with crime. They describe an emerging trend to apply the latest advances in computer technology and software to law enforcement. Much like a doctor diagnosing and prescribing treatment for a patient, these systems offer expert advice to law enforcement officials and practitioners.

Expert systems are computer programs that simulate the way experts solve problems and improve performance in selected areas. In the criminal justice environment, expert systems are now used to support crime-solving, decision-making, training, and program planning and design. They contain the best knowledge available about law enforcement issues and practices and serve as consultants and advisers to law enforcement officials.

The practice of using experts as consultants or advisers is not high tech, nor is the methodology of artificial intelligence. What is relatively new is blend of practice and technology in the form of expert systems to help solve actual problems. Artificial intelligence (AI) has its roots in the 1950's when scientists began to research the thinking process of humans and use machines to simulate that process. It was not until the 1970's that useful applications of this research for problem solving in the form of expert systems made their way out of the laboratories and into use.

Expert systems first found applications in the research community. The original rule-based system was MYCIN, developed at Stanford University as a research project for medical diagnosis (Shortliffe 1976). Today expert systems can be found in such diverse fields as mineral exploration, chemistry, medical diagnosis, tax accounting, and management.

The most important features of expert systems and those that distinguish them from other systems are:

* Their methods of capturing and representing knowledge to aid in problem solving.
* Their ability to make inferences about unobserved phenomena and suggest what would happen under uncertain conditions.
* Their capacity to capture and retain the memory and history of an institution for as long as information about a subject matter and expertise is required.
* Their capability to provide realistic and intelligent training and dissemination of information to all levels of personnel.

Because of these characteristics, properly designed expert systems are imaginative, accurate, and efficient in problem solving; cost-effective, flexible, and dynamic; capable of being started with a relatively modest investment and of being expanded and updated; and permanent, retaining a large pool of institutional knowledge and experience that can be easily disseminated to others (Waterman 1986: 7).

LAW ENFORCEMENT INTEREST IN EXPERT SYSTEMS

Although expert systems have been used in many fields, they have only recently received attention by law enforcement and criminal justice agencies. This is due in part to the newness of the technology and in part to the scarcity of practitioners in the criminal justice community who are aware of the potential of these systems and understand the methodology of implementing them. Despite these limitations, the potential value of the technology has been recognized, especially by the federal government.

To date, much of the work at the federal level has focused on developing profiles of various types of offenders. The Federal Bureau of Investigation (FBI), through its Center for the Analysis of Violent Crimes, is developing profiles about killers who commit certain types of murders. Additionally, its Big Floyd system tracks the movements and activities of suspected organized crime members. Others interested in the profiling ability of these systems are the Drug Enforcement Administration (DEA), the Internal Revenue Service (IRS), the Treasury Department, and the Environmental Protection Agency (EPA). In fact, the Office of Technology Assessment in 1986 identified sixteen agencies using some form of computer profiling primarily for law enforcement purposes.

Profiling has been the primary focus at the federal level because of the expert system's ability to distill large amounts of data and form profiles based on known or assumed relationships between behavior and personal characteristics. Thus, the IRS can profile the likely cheat on income taxes, the DEA can profile drug runners, and the EPA can identify likely polluters.

At the local law enforcement level, applications of expert systems to date have been concentrated in three major areas: real-time decision-making, crime-solving, training, and program planning and design. These general application areas are worthy of discussion since each has substantially different characteristics and highlights different issues.

Real-Time Decision-Making

Many situations in law enforcement are stressful, particularly those that require real-time decision-making. Most notable are computer-aided dispatch (CAD), 911 systems, and emergency medical service (EMS). In these areas, choosing one action among alternatives largely depends on the information presented and the experience and training of the decision-makers.

Although the choices available to a dispatcher are not extensive (for example, to respond immediately to a call for service, to delay police response until a more appropriate time, or not to respond at all), the type and quantity of information available to the dispatcher is highly variable. This is especially true when emergency calls are received from distraught citizens or the activity level in the area is quite high.

The choices are not always equal in priority either. In 911 systems, for example, the operator's role is a crucial one, demanding an accurate diagnosis of emergency calls and the ability to ask for the appropriate information. Most police departments use a three-level priority system: priority one involves life-threatening experiences requiring immediate response; level two includes property-threatening situations that will be serviced immediately if there are no priority one calls; and level three are minor violations serviced only when

resources are available. The decisions are also constrained by
other external factors over which the dispatcher may have little
control, such as the availability of vehicles and their location.

The major problem faced in these types of applications is
developing a response-allocation model that reacts to various
resource allocation strategies efficiently and effectively.
Richard Larson at MIT attempts to "marry" expert systems with
operations research programs by dividing the service region into
small geographical "atoms" that can be assigned to a patrol unit's
beat and be deployed according to the response model (Larson
1978).

Since the systems are in real-time, the validity of the
allocation model is critical to operations, more so than in any
other application area.   It has to consider, in addition to
availability of the responding units, such factors as travel time,
in-service times, special needs (such as bilingual officers), and
even the fatigue levels of the responding units. A CAD system
developed for the Delaware State Police (Ratledge 1988) takes
these priorities into consideration. The expert system provides
the category and the priority for the call for service to the
dispatcher, suggests the appropriate vehicle to respond, and then
may suggest that other action be taken, such as to hold a unit on
overtime or shift backup units.

By their very nature, expert systems strengthen the
consistency and uniformity of the decision-making process. This
is particularly important since there are often multiple operators,
with varying degrees of experience, handling different types of
calls.   The system brings objectivity and comprehensiveness to
decision-making. For example, if there are three dispatchers
with varying degrees of experience, they should, with the help of
the system, come up with the same or similar decisions in
approximately the same amount of time. Further, there are real
possibilities for extending the range of decisions that a
dispatcher makes to include tactical realignment of resources
currently deployed, holding resources that might otherwise go
off duty, and identifying the need for specialized resources that
are not deployed but are on call. By capturing the decisions
made over time, the expert system may also be able to modify
itself (that is, learn) and provide suggestions for modifying the
longer-run deployment of resources.

For real-time decision-making systems, the critical factors
for success lie in three areas: (1) a well-defined set of decisions,
(2) the specification of most of the conditions that the user is
likely to encounter, and (3) the quality of the interface between
the user and the system.

The relevant decisions are those that the decision-maker would not normally solve in a few seconds. The decision to dispatch car(s) to a call for service takes into consideration a number of factors that make decision-making difficult, however, it is not so difficult that it would take two hours to make the decision. In essence, the problem area has to be bounded so it can be solved quickly.

The expertise needed to build a body of knowledge that captures all decisions taken under a multitude of circumstances may require only a few of the most experienced persons. These experts must be able to articulate not only the full range of circumstances likely to occur but also to specify the expected response that reflects the policy of the agency.

The user interface is critical in real-time systems because more often than not, the advice offered is based on incomplete information. The system must evaluate the information for sufficiency and request additional specific information from the user. At the same time, the system must be able to explain to the user why it has suggested a certain course of action. The basic criterion for a successful system is that it can make decisions acceptable to the most experienced person within desirable time limits. When these conditions are met, local jurisdictions derive substantial benefits from the application of expert systems in this situation.

Crime-Solving

Unless the criminal is captured at the scene of the crime, crime-solving requires a fair degree of experience, analytic capability, and creativity. The benefits accruing from the application of expert systems can be substantial since individuals possessing all of these characteristics are often in short supply. In police departments, this expertise most often is found within a select set of experienced detectives or investigators.

The first local application of expert systems to crime-solving relied on the expertise of detectives and crime lab road technicians in the Baltimore County (Maryland) Police Department (BCPD). This project was conducted in conjunction with the Devon and Cornwall Constabulary in Exeter, England, and was supported by funding from the U.S. Department of Justice, the National Institute of Justice, (grant number 87-IJ-CX-0019) and the Bureau of Justice Assistance (grant numbers 87-SD-CX-K088 and 88-MU-CX-K003). The Jefferson Institute for Justice Studies (a nonprofit organization located in Washington, D.C.) directed the installation of the expert system and will soon implement tailored systems in three other police departments (Jacoby et al. 1988).

Residential burglaries were selected as the focus because they are one of the most pervasive and troublesome crimes in the United States. They constitute the bulk of felonious crimes affecting millions of citizens, and are also the most difficult to solve. In Baltimore County and in most other urban areas, the arrest rate hovers annually at, or under, 15 percent.

Solving burglaries is a chronic and persistent problem. There are rarely witnesses to the incident and physical evidence in the form of recovered stolen property or fingerprints is usually not available. This lack of evidence coupled with the personnel rotation policy and early retirement of most departments, which riddles the ranks of experienced detectives, leads to a poor solution rate.

The expert system for residential burglaries uses the combined knowledge and expertise of burglary detectives and crime lab technicians to identify likely suspects based on characteristics of the burglary and the behavior of the suspect. It creates a behavioral fingerprint which is matched to a file of known or previously arrested burglars. The output is relatively straightforward. The expert system produces: (1) a list of suspects and a scale measuring their likelihood of being the offender; (2) messages that will aid the investigators, such as, "This is probably domestic related"; and (3) signatures that identify a suspect because of some unique behavioral pattern.

This system produces profiles of burglars based on their behavior at the scene. The profiles, coupled with other aspects of the crime, are matched to a file of *known* offenders. In this respect, although profiling is used as part of the matching process, the output identifies by name the most likely candidates from a universe. (There is an inherent limitation to this system since first-time offenders who have never been arrested will not be in the database.) Even if no match is found or the scale scores are too low, the expert system provides a general profile of the burglar from the characteristics of the crime. For example, a profile might state that the burglar is most likely a white, male, juvenile, who lives nearby and is a drug abuser.

The residential burglary expert system is different from the pattern-recognition matching systems like PATRIC, which operated in the Los Angeles Police Department in the early 1970's (Government Data Systems 1973; Jackson 1976). Modus Operandi (M.O.) matching systems initially required one-on-one matching of data elements. For example, if a burglar cut glass to gain entry, as part of the identification match, the system assumed that he cut glass every time. In time, these systems evolved into much more sophisticated pattern-matching systems that integrated data analysis with the crime analysis functions of law enforcement agencies.

In contrast to pattern matching, expert systems have the ability to make inferences about unobserved characteristics that serve to limit the possible subset culprits for investigation. For example, cutting glass or using vise grips indicates an experienced burglar. The expert system then looks for experienced burglars as part of its matching process.

To make inferences, the residential burglary system needs knowledge. This knowledge is in the form of a rule base that represents the knowledge of the experts (detectives) in the form of if-then statements. For example, if the glass is cut, then the burglar is experienced. Or, if the property taken includes junk jewelry and teenage miscellany, then the suspect is a juvenile. Developing a knowledge base that articulates the thought processes of detectives and investigators is the foundation of an expert system.

Unlike applications in the CAD system, which may rely on the expertise of a few, crime-solving applications are likely to be based on a body of knowledge acquired from many. As a result, expert systems are only as good as the combined and accumulated knowledge of all detectives. It is clear that there is no single supercop or expert in burglaries, a veritable Sherlock Holmes. Burglaries differ geographically, thereby giving one group of detectives a knowledge base and expertise that is different from another group operating in another area. For example, in Baltimore County, East Side detectives had a different set of knowledge from West Side detectives. Since all knowledge is relevant to the system, one detective alone cannot speak for an entire force.

The collective knowledge and expertise held within the system represents the institutional memory of detectives who have ever served that force. Detectives may retire, be promoted, or leave, but their expertise and knowledge is retained for as long as it is relevant. In crime-solving applications, this is particularly important since offenders may be convicted, sentenced, and become unavailable for long periods of time. The expert system's memory remains intact however, and when the offender is eventually released from prison and is ready to resume his or her chosen career, the expert system's memory is available and ready to help a new detective or an older one who has forgotten the pattern.

The use of expert systems to assist in the solution of residential burglaries is only one possible application within the general area of crime-solving, but it illustrates some of the conditions that must be met for these systems to work. These applications assume the existence of repeat offenders who have a high frequency of criminal activity and whose behavior is generally consistent and capable of being classified or categorized by experts in crime-solving. Future applications in crime-solving may focus on commercial burglaries, commercial robberies, assaults, and arson. Crimes that occur infrequently or have little behavioral information are less likely targets for an expert system.

Training

Training and instruction are somewhat removed from the operational environment, but the application of expert systems in these areas shows great potential. Experience has already shown the value of computer-aided instruction (CAI) and computer-based training (CBT). These applications, however, have traditionally been deterministic; that is, they follow a set script. Truly effective training demands a sense of realism and thus a more dynamic and flexible approach.

The fact that expert systems contain a body of knowledge drawn from the best in the business makes them immediately relevant to training. While the conversion of an operational system to a training system is not without cost, it provides an important benefit from the department's investment in creating the original system. Expert systems already contain the necessary knowledge and have the ability to explain their reasoning processes. Expert systems provide a foundation for personalizing training experiences and bringing the user's real world into a workshop. Only the user interface and printed materials must be changed or added. When converted, the training version should act much like simulators with which we are all familiar.

The primary goals of a training program are to ensure uniformity in operations and decision-making when the trainee enters the real world and to standardize the acquisition of and use of relevant and complete information by transferring practice on the streets to the classroom. The value of using expert systems in training as well as operations is apparent and was clearly demonstrated in Baltimore County's residential burglary project. The statements and rules gathered from the experts provided the basis for an investigators' training course, identified the data needed, and emphasized the need for comprehensive and uniform data collection.

Program Planning and Design

Over the past two decades, federal and local law enforcement and prosecution agencies have given top priority to developing programs that focus on special offender groups, such as career criminals, repeat offenders, drug abusers, and violent juvenile offenders. To assist jurisdictions in developing these programs, training and technical assistance has been provided by the Bureau of Justice Assistance (BJA). These programs have been especially effective in helping local criminal justice agencies design and plan programs tailored to the characteristics of their environment that will satisfy the policies or goals of the agency.

Technical assistance programs tap a pool of expert consultants and experienced practitioners who are usually sent as advisers to the local jurisdiction. They assist the agencies in designing programs consistent with their goals and make recommendations for the subsequent steps needed to reach operational status.

The design and operation of successful career criminal programs, for example, are based on a careful consideration of a number of factors, including the legislative environment, court procedures and rules, the structure and functioning of the criminal justice system, and the policies and politics of the various agencies. The interface between varied criminal justice agencies often is the key to whether the program is successful. If police and prosecutors in a jurisdiction do not cooperate, establishing a repeat offender program is far more difficult than in jurisdictions where they do. The program design and its operating procedures are developed by experts who offer to the jurisdiction knowledge about which combinations of procedures will best meet the specific goals of the program directors while avoiding conflicts within the criminal justice environment.

Not all agencies can afford to hire consultants, and many agencies do not have the ability to diagnose their own situations in order to make improvements to existing operations. Even with substantial BJA funding, there are not enough resources to meet the demand for this type of service. Training is expensive, teachers or experts are in short supply, and no single prescriptive program model can satisfy the variety of environments within which career criminal programs and others like them can operate. Manuals discussing the issues and setting forth basic principles are important, but they are not flexible enough to produce the tailoring to satisfy individual program needs.

It is because of this need for flexibility that expert systems find a fertile environment. They are capable of capturing the knowledge of the different ways programs can be designed and implemented and then tailoring one for a specific jurisdiction. In effect, the expert system captures the knowledge of the technical assistance consultants and allows a jurisdiction to design its own program based on the knowledge contained in the system and its own environment.

An expert system for career criminal-repeat offender programs is under development by the Jefferson Institute for Justice Studies. Supported by the BJA, this system will allow local law enforcement and prosecution agencies to plan and design a program based on their priorities yet suited to the criminal justice environment within which the program will have to operate (BJA grant number 87-SA-CX-K082).

The system allows the user (police and/or prosecutor) to select the goals and objectives of the program, (e.g., incapacitation) and designate the type of program (prearrest or postarrest) and the director (police or prosecutor). Through a series of questions, it creates a program design consistent with the environment, court procedures, jail capacity, and other criminal justice resources and policies. If the user selects inconsistent procedures or inconsistent or problematic designs, the expert system points out this problem and suggests alternative approaches. This system is highly interactive with the users and at completion, it produces a program plan for their review and consideration.

The purpose of this project is to take advantage of the relatively low distribution costs of this software, thus extending the ability of BJA to provide more training and assistance to state and local government units at lower cost. If this objective can be met, the potential use of expert systems for other federal assistance programs will extend far beyond criminal justice applications and will directly influence most types of technical and program design assistance offered by the federal government.

ARE EXPERT SYSTEMS WORTH THE EFFORT?

The effectiveness of expert systems in criminal justice is not as yet proven. One may therefore legitimately question their value to criminal justice agencies and law enforcement.

First, why not rely on human expertise as we have done in the past? What is so valuable about using computer techniques to simulate human reasoning? One answer is that the knowledge contained in an expert system is permanent. It will not fade or diminish. It can be transferred from one human to another by copying a file or program. It can be documented in a clear, straightforward manner. Therefore, expert systems produce more consistent, reproducible results than does human expertise because it is not subject to stress, distractions, or other emotional situations (Waterman 1986: 13). Further, by definition, the system contains the knowledge of experts who have more expertise than the user of the system.

This is not to say that human expertise should or will be eliminated from problem solving. There still is a vital need for the expert's creativity, intuition, learning ability, and commonsense knowledge, all difficult to transfer to a computer. Much like the residential burglary system that identifies likely suspects, it is the human (detective) work element that ultimately leads to the successful outcome--in this case, the arrest and prosecution of the offender. Expert systems are meant to assist the user and allow the human expert to focus on the more difficult factors that will help solve the problem.

If a problem appears to lend itself to the application of expert systems and one is developed, a set of practical questions is introduced.

Does it work? Are the experts who lent their knowledge to the system and the users of the system satisfied with its help? In the residential burglary system, does it identify suspects, who are then arrested? Even a 2 percentage point increase in burglary arrests will have a greater impact on the safety of the community than the number implies because of the high frequency of criminal activity associated with the offender.

Are the real-time operational decisions made by dispatchers consistent with those that would have been made by the most experienced personnel?

Was the program design produced by the expert system useful? Was it implemented by the local agencies?

Expert systems should help the user, but their role is advisory and supportive. That is the primary and only reason for their existence.

Is it worth the effort? The development of an expert system is much more difficult than creating conventional programs. Good experts are hard to find; sometimes extracting knowledge from them is even more difficult. Integrating a system like the residential burglary or the CAD into the operations of an agency requires not only a large expenditure of effort and time, but it also has an impact on and changes other aspects of management and operations that might not have been considered. For example, it may change the forms and reporting procedures in the agency. Or, more subtly, it may shift power from staff to line functions. The fact that the experts in the police department are detectives, not majors or commanders, may create subtle but real conflicts in the maintenance, direction, and even expansion of the system.

Finally, although expert systems are costly to develop, they are relatively inexpensive to operate. Their high developmental and testing costs may be more than offset by the increased understanding that the agency has of its own functions especially those related to training.

Are there other benefits that accrue indirectly from the system? Not all benefits may be direct. The BCPD is interested in redesigning its investigator's training course to take advantage of the knowledge and expertise articulated by the detectives. It is also assessing the use of other, non-sworn personnel (such as crime lab technicians or public service officers) for data collection. Because of the existing Citizen Oriented Police Enforcement program, it is also interested in assessing the impact of this system on the public's and victim's perception of safety.

The advantages of expert systems can be summarized as follows:

> 1. They permit non-experts to do the work of experts.
> 2. They improve productivity by increasing the quality and quantity of output.
> 3. They permit new kinds of problems to be solved, making the computer more useful.
> 4. They capture and store valuable knowledge that might be lost.
> 5. They make expert knowledge available to a wider audience, thus increasing the problem-solving ability of more people (Frenzel 1987: 73).

ORGANIZATIONAL IMPLICATIONS

The major difference between the traditional management information systems and expert systems is one of emphasis. The systems of the 1960's and 1970's managed information, collected data, validated the input, and queried the output. In only some instances were the data coded to reflect specific detail about how a person looked at a problem. A prominent example is the PROMIS system, which in its original version asked for the prosecutor's subjective assessment of the priority of the case for prosecution (Jacoby 1972). Another common example was the creation of tickler files that provided court dockets or produced timely notifications for police witness schedules.

The difference between expert systems and more traditional data processing lies in the ability of expert systems to extend the usefulness of the databases to make judgments and suggest what people should do next. These systems operate on knowledge gathered from experts. That knowledge base allows for more effective use of data that the departments already have and suggests changes to that database. These systems also have the ability to deal with imprecise, fuzzy, and uncertain data.

It is this last characteristic that strongly differentiates traditional information systems from expert systems. Expert systems not only extend the data base into a knowledge base but also use certainty factors to reflect uncertainty about data and conclusions. More important, these certainties can change and evolve as more knowledge is added to the system. For example, detectives may estimate that 90 percent of the time a criminal who uses force to gain entry is a juvenile; after collecting enough data, they may change the rate to 80 percent.

Traditional management information systems are generally not used to make inferences about other unknown data elements. The residential burglary expert system, which uses a traditional database, can view the nature of the offense and provide estimates of the characteristics of the perpetrator even if he was not observed at the scene.

It is the ability of expert systems to operate as inference machines that provides criminal justice with new and powerful assistance in its operations and management. Much of the criminal justice environment already operates under conditions of uncertainty, ranging from the likelihood of being arrested to the likelihood of being convicted. Expert systems reflect this process by using uncertainty in a systematic, structured fashion, derived from experience and fact patterns, and producing for the practitioner suggestions for alternative courses of action.

The expert system will never replace the expert. The fact that four or five suspects may be identified as likely offenders in an unsolved crime does not relieve the detective from obtaining the evidence or the prosecutor from obtaining the conviction. Programs designed by expert systems have to be implemented, and the dispatchers will still have to judge the advice offered. These systems are tools, not solutions.

To support this new approach to problem solving, the commitment of the agency head is essential, along with the establishment of a top-level project team that can provide management and coordination as needed on a continuous basis. The project coordinator must be creative and experienced in problem solving and accommodation. Flexibility and experimentation are the keys to the successful implementation of the project.

The demand on resources will continue long after the system is operational. It will be felt in monitoring and refining new reporting procedures and in maintaining the system. These systems utilize sophisticated equipment and complex software. One cannot expect police department personnel to be trained in the software and systems support required. Additional funds will have to be set aside for this specialized training or for the use of contractual services.

Similarly, there will be a need for ongoing evaluation and monitoring. After the initial enthusiasm and support wanes, there should be in-house capacity to monitor the use and results and record where dissatisfaction is occurring and why. The investment is too great to let the system fail because of correctable faults.

CONCLUSION

Decisions to develop expert systems should not be made without careful consideration of the technical aspects of the system and the impact on the organization and personnel. Most important, those who are interested in criminal justice applications must understand that expert systems are not black boxes that a jurisdiction can buy, plug in, and get results. Simply having enough money to buy an expert system will not guarantee that the product will work. Expert systems require expertise in many areas; a black box will not suffice for these applications.

Drawing from the experience in the 1970's when systems were installed based on more promise than performance and recognizing that similar pressures will grow in this area, it is important that the users of expert systems form a network that will provide mutual support and advice based on experience. Expert systems are still in their infancy for law enforcement and criminal justice applications, their utilization needs as much protection as possible.

2
EXPERT SYSTEMS AND POLICING ISSUES

The problems facing today's progressive police chiefs bear little resemblance to those of their predecessors, even those of only two decades past. In the late 1960's and early 1970's, talk was about the "war on crime," jurisdictional consolidation, standards, and goals. Today the vocabulary includes terms like *fiscal stress, resource allocation, crime prevention,* and *community-oriented and problem-solving policing.* Terms like *computer-aided dispatching, computer-based training, mobile dispatch terminals, laptop computers, automated fingerprint identification, database management, artificial intelligence,* and *expert systems* suggest how complex and pervasive the technology has become in only a few years. Programs involving repeat offenders, organized criminals, asset seizures and forfeitures clandestine lab task forces, computer crimes, and even international terrorism indicate the high degree of sophistication that is now part of modern policing. The complexities introduced by the law and technology alone have often strained police resources to their limits and have hampered the ability of police to provide the quality of services to the public that they desire. Thus, serious questions have been raised about setting priorities for service in a department constrained by fixed resources.

Despite new legislation and advanced technology, there is an unsettling, and often discouraging, sameness about the issues and problems confronting today's chief of police. They still center on training, personnel management, and the delivery of services to the community. Within each of these areas is hidden a complex array of issues and problems that have become increasingly complicated as society becomes more urbanized and technologically advanced.

Over the years, chiefs of police have looked to science and technology to help them provide services more efficiently and effectively. One can hardly imagine how crimes were solved before the discovery of fingerprints as identifiers. Imagine what the genetic matching capability of DNA fingerprinting will bring to this activity! Science has found a receptive home in policing, and this book reflects that interest by discussing how expert systems can be applied to law enforcement activities.

In this chapter, we examine some of the critical areas in policing that have the potential for degrading and reducing police effectiveness but can be controlled with the assistance of AI and expert systems. Specifically we look at the core of police problems encountered in command and control, crime-solving, and personnel management. We examine how expert systems can support some of the activities in each of these areas, indicate some benefits, and identify some of the policy issues that they may produce, even unwittingly.

COMMAND AND CONTROL

Command and control refers to the department's ability to deploy its varied resources in the best possible way to meet the diverse demands made upon those resources. Those demands include responding to calls for service, conducting investigations, working in crime prevention and other activities. The objective is to balance the use of these scarce resources and' to make the best possible action decisions based on timely and relevant information. Command and control systems, whether manual or automated, are the cornerstone of a police department. They have the ability to make a police department more effective in responding to crime and other order-maintenance problems. In a larger sense, the quality of justice in communities is tied to the success or failure of the police department's command and control function.

The objectives of command and control systems are basically threefold:

1. Improve the effectiveness of police in utilizing their resources in responding to calls for service, maintaining order, and conducting other resource hungry activities.
2. Furnish officers in the field with timely and relevant data so they can make best possible decisions.

3. Increase uniformity and consistency in decision making throughout the force area.

Each of these objectives will be affected by the introduction of expert system technology much as they were in the past when other technological advances were adopted by the departments.

Computer-Aided Dispatching and Response Time

In 1967, the President's Commission on Law Enforcement and Administration of Justice stressed the effects that police command and control systems had on response times: namely the positive relationship between apprehension rates and response time (President's Commission on Law Enforcement and Administration of Justice 1967).

In the commission's task force report on science and technology, command and control problems involving radio congestion and other issues that limited police response time to calls for service were discussed, and recommendations were set forth.   One recommendation was to apply the power of the computer technology to the problem (Colton 1978).

Computer technology in a sense revolutionized policing in the late 1960's and early 1970's by offering police a more efficient means of dealing with simultaneous requests for service.   The meteoric rise in emergency calls for service prompted police managers to take a closer look at how their agency could more effectively respond to these new demands (Doering   and   Clapp 1976).   Sparked by urban riots and increasing disorder in cities, the original emergency command and control centers were created. They bear little resemblance to the highly automated, rapid-response communications centers of today.

CAD   systems   automated   the   call   processing   and dispatching functions.   Initially they were limited because they could not locate police vehicles. This led to the development of automated vehicle monitoring and automatic vehicle location systems.   The emergency 911 telephone systems, mobile and portable digital terminals, and high-tech radio equipment quickly followed and are now integral parts of communication centers in many police departments throughout the nation (Colton 1978, 1983).

Today the law enforcement literature is filled with articles highlighting innovative communication systems that have made the department work load more manageable. In Lakeland, Florida, patrol cars are being equipped with computers to store "car hot sheets, wanted person lists, street maps and a telephone directory" (Clede 1986: 38). In Dayton, Ohio, spoken words are recorded on hard disks (Law and Order 1988); in San Jose, California, officers can immediately see the status and location of all other officers in the precinct through a digital terminal (Clede 1986); in St. Petersburg, Florida, cars are equipped with laptop computers for report writing, cellular telephones have been placed in some patrol cars, and a computer system to allow officers to draw accidents on a computer screen at the scene is being developed (Stone 1988). Since St. Petersburg, Florida's pioneering use of laptop computers, police departments in Colorado, Texas, and Kentucky have added them to their operations division (Birchler 1988).

Information for Decision Making and Action

Reiss (1971) has defined two basic types of law enforcement decisions made by officers to maintain order and control in society: proactive and reactive. A proactive decision is an action taken by the police officer without a dispatcher's aid. A reactive decision is one in which the patrol officer responds to a call initiated by the dispatcher. The command and control function encompasses both types, although historically more attention has been given to the reactive decisions.

Both types of decisions are important to the broad issue of command and control because they are the clearest, observable reflection of department policy and procedure (Jacoby 1982). Decisions, however, are made with varying levels of certainty (Gottfredson and Gottfredson 1980) depending on the existence of clear-cut policies and procedures and the sufficiency of the information provided to the decision-maker. Poor decisions are more likely to occur when information is incomplete, inaccurate, or out of date; timely and complete data contribute to better decisions. For this reason, a significant area of concern to command and control is the ability to furnish patrol officers with the best information available. Automated information systems are especially suited to this task.

In Iowa, a multi-agency computer system is hooked up to four different police departments. This network enables these agencies to communicate using a common database. "This communication ability not only allows shared information and files to be accessed by all four agencies, but also provides each agency access to the state IOWA system and the federal network" (Smith 1986: 34).

The St. Petersburg, Florida, Police Department has cellular telephones "where the work is done" (Stone 1988: 23). With the car telephones, officers can talk directly to 90 percent of the homes and just about all the businesses in St. Petersburg. In Dayton, Ohio, in-car keyboard data terminals (Motorola KDTS) give police officers access to data banks to see if a person encountered is on probation, has previously been involved with stolen property, or is wanted (Law and Order 1988).

These examples represent the traditional reliance that law enforcement agencies have placed on the use of communications technology. The speed with which police departments adapt to the latest innovations bears strong witness to their need for accurate and timely information.

Uniform and Consistent Decision Making

High-tech applications have made the work of police officers and dispatchers more efficient, but they still require persons to make decisions. Decisions require discretion. The discretionary decisions police make daily have a profound impact on the quality and distribution of justice meted out (Cole 1983). A major difficulty all agencies encounter is controlling the use of discretion and ensuring that decisions made are consistent with the policy of the agency (Jacoby 1980).

In the decision-making world of the dispatcher, the consequences of inadequate information or experience are clear. Automated equipment can handle the calls efficiently, but it is the decision-making process which sets priorities, dispatches, and monitors calls so adjustments can be made as the situation changes. Even this decision-making process can be stretched beyond belief when it has to cope with major emergencies such as the one that occurred in Washington, D.C. during the evening rush hour of 1982 when, in the midst of a blinding snow storm, a plane crashed into the 14th Street Bridge and a subway accident caused multiple fatalities and injuries.

When the decision-making process involves multiple decision-makers, even though they are working together in the same communication center, there is little assurance that all will make the same decision since their experience and training vary. The life saved may very well depend on the experience level of the dispatcher. The underlying goal of dispatch systems is to optimize the uniformity of decisions.

"A command and control system has the inherent capability of rapid and complete information assembly, decision-making and execution" (Doering and Clapp 1976: 94). One significant problem is how to incorporate information on the current state of the CAD system into a real-time decision-making process so that dispatchers make a series of decisions simultaneously or instantaneously (Lee and Larson 1984). For example, if there are ten dispatchers using the same database and two require a particular resource, how do we guarantee that the most important call gets the allocation. The system must be able to evaluate any pending requests on a more complex basis than first come - first serve. In fact, having resources available is not a sufficient condition to allocate resources to respond. This technical problem extends into the policy area when a chief of police is coordinating a system that allocates resources in an intergovernmental environment. When state, county, and local police are tied together with the same system, intergovernmental policies and coordination priorities must be established and integrated with local operations if these systems are to be successful.

A New Approach with Expert Systems

Despite all of the advances in software and equipment, the key to the success of a command and control function is the people who make the final decisions. It is the link between the information system and the human ability to make inferences about the information provided that is of interest. Expert systems using a knowledge base in addition to the typical data base, can simulate the inferential thought process of the human and impact all of the primary objectives of the command and control system.

For example, the patrolman in Dayton who queries his in-car terminal for information about a suspect or a location can make a better decision than an officer without access to this information. Add an expert system component to this capability, and the patrolman will be provided with advice in addition to information. For example, the expert system would know that under certain circumstances (e.g., past calls for service from that location, where violence had been encountered, and where the domestic scene was particularly troublesome), patrol should not respond without backup, and it would flash this message to the officer. The expert system thus has the ability to capture the knowledge gained from street experience and pass it on to others. It is important to note that some of these situations may be obvious to the experienced officer and others may be part of S.O.P. However, in more subtle situations, the expert system is a helpful reminder to the inexperienced and the overworked alike.

Similarly, if any one of the state police dispatchers in Delaware is equally likely to receive emergency requests for service, it is important that the same factors be included in their decision about the appropriate response. An expert system that captures the experience and reasoning of the most experienced dispatchers could work in tandem with the CAD system. It would ensure that the same information is collected by any dispatcher regardless of experience level or skill. Then it would recommend allocation and assignment decisions based on its collective experience and expertise. It would, in fact, reproduce the decisions that would be made by the best dispatcher.

Expert systems are not the final solution to command and control problems. Even with their ability to capture the knowledge and thought processes of the experts, they can work only within narrow problem areas. For example, if an action decision by the patrol officer has to take into consideration not only the nature of the suspect and the location of the incident but also the actions of an undercover task force operation, the expert system would not necessarily be privy to the undercover operations, and, hence, would make its decisions without considering this crucial information in its decision-making process. Then again, the typical street cop may not always be privy to such activities either. While the command and control system should "know" about the allocation of resources to that activity, it is unlikely that anything more than a warning message could be generated for the dispatcher. More complex responses would have to be generated by expanding the knowledge base of the expert system.

Notwithstanding the future of expert systems, the present already suggests that attention has to be given to the issue of how to keep and enhance the independent thinking and decision making of law enforcement officers. It would be unfortunate if the best minds in policing were tuned out because of an overreliance on the expert system. One could envision a dispatcher or officer justifying a decision or action "because the computer said so." No matter how carefully designed a system is, there will always be problems. Adding an expert system component does not guarantee that the information provided by the expert is error free. In some instances, the expert system may give poor advice just as humans do because its knowledge base is wrong or incomplete. In fact one of the most pervasive problems with human dispatchers is their lack of experience and their faulty reasoning process. Whether we are dealing with human or computer dispatchers the limitations of the knowledge base has to be recognized, accounted for, and monitored.

The limits of expert systems are obvious to those who develop application packages for command and control but not always to users of the systems. Once expert systems are in place and operational, their deleterious effects on independent thought and critical analysis of events may not be clear. Subtle reliance on computer decision making has to be guarded against. The department will have to take an active interest in supporting and recognizing the legitimacy of intuition, creativity, and criticism. One must never forget that the role of expert systems is to give opinions or offer advice; they do not, and should not, have the final voice in decision-making.

CRIME-SOLVING

Police activities in the United States are conducted for four basic purposes: order maintenance, information collection, service, and law enforcement. Although the majority of the activities are directed to the first three functions (Wilson 1971), it is the law enforcement and crime-solving aspects of policing that are given the most attention by the public.

Studies of calls for service dispatch records show that patrol officers spend about one-third of their time on specific assignments. The remaining two-thirds is spent on general patrol, officer-initiated contacts with citizens (mostly traffic stops), citizen-initiated encounters, and personal business (Boydstun and Sherry 1975; Boydstun et al. 1977; Tien et al. 1978). There is substantial variation in the amount of time patrol officers spend responding to assigned calls, and the averages conceal wide variations by beat, shift, and jurisdiction (Whitaker et al. 1982).

Clearly the commonly held view of police as crime-solvers is rarely mirrored in reality. For the most part, crime is involved in only a minority of police calls (Whitaker et al. 1982). The most common instigation of legal proceedings is not arrests but the issuance of traffic tickets. In fact, Brian Forst (Forst et al. 1978) reported in his study of the Washington Metropolitan Police Department that 46 percent of all sworn officers made no arrests in 1974.

Even if we look to detectives and investigators to shoulder primary crime-solving responsibility, Whitaker notes that "criminal investigators do not solve most of the crimes reported to police. They do not even identify the suspects in most of the crimes which police consider cleared. . . . Most cases are cleared by patrol officers who make arrests at or near the scene of the crime or who obtain identification of suspects from witnesses or victims during their initial investigation of the crime" (Whitaker et al. 1982: 73). Investigators spend much of their time gathering and processing evidence for the prosecution of suspects already identified and apprehended.

A study of detective time in Kansas City, Missouri, by Peter Greenwood and colleagues (1975) indicated that detectives spent about 56 percent of their time on case work, defined as activities related to specific reported crimes. Another 14 percent was spent on general administrative activities and 2 percent on general surveillance, crime prevention, and other service activities not related to specific cases (29 percent of their time was not accounted for by the data system employed).

Although the public's perception of police as crime-solvers is distorted, the interest, if not the activities of law enforcement agencies, does not conflict with this perception. There has never been any argument about the importance of this function, and there have been large investments of time and money to improve the crime-solving capabilities of law enforcement. The purpose of these investments is made clear by three sets of activities that, ideally, are achieved for every crime:

1. Collecting and retaining accurate information on offenses that aid the investigation.
2. Identifying and apprehending the suspect.
3. Providing evidence and information about the incident and arrests for prosecution.

Within an environment characterized by scarce resources and a high-volume demand for services, the test of good police managers is their efficient and effective use of personnel in solving crimes and apprehending criminals. "The amount of time spent on various types of crimes depends on three factors: the frequency with which the type of crime is reported, the difficulty detectives have in clearing cases of that type, and the priority which police attach to crimes of that type" (Whitaker et al. 1982: 75).

Crimes against property are the most difficult crimes to solve because there is little likelihood that a suspect will be arrested at the scene, identified by a witness, or leave some unique evidence. These are the three most prevalent reasons for arrests and clearances that Greenwood found in his studies (Greenwood et al. 1975), and they have been substantiated by other researchers (Bloch and Bell 1976; Conklin 1972) in their studies of Rochester, New York, and Boston, Massachusetts, respectively.

Burglaries have been particularly difficult to solve. As a result, it is not surprising to see innovative case-screening procedures developed for police departments to allocate investigative resources. The Stanford Research Institute (SRI) developed one of the first models that selected burglary cases with the greatest chance of being solved (Greenberg et al. 1973) based on data from Alameda County, California. Other felony case assignment models for case screening were used in Rochester, New York (Bloch and Bell 1976), and in Multnomah County, Oregon (Brand and Koroloff 1976). The SRI model was replicated in twenty-six police departments in the late 1970's (Eck 1979). The concept of managing criminal investigations (MCI) has been adopted by several more police departments since the Eck report found that case-screening instruments are significantly efficient.

MCI systems provide police managers with guidelines for assigning cases based on their likely solvability to patrol, detectives, or investigators. The screening factors collected during the preliminary investigation phase determine who will be responsible for further investigative work, if any. Thus, patrol officers can follow up on easily solvable cases, allowing investigators to concentrate on more difficult cases. MCI was not designed to meet the objectives of crime solving but rather to screen and give priority to the investigative work in the agency. As such, it is a management tool, not an operational system.

More operational are systems that identify likely suspects based on some other matching evidence. The latest technological developments have focused on automated fingerprint identification systems (AFIS), DNA matching, and M.O. matching systems. As their names indicate, each attempts to match various types of evidence to an individual.

AFIS gave law enforcement agencies their first opportunity to use a high-speed, investigative tool for the fingerprint identification of suspects. Sold by a number of vendors, these systems identify suspects based on partial, latent fingerprints (they also identify from rolled ink impressions). The latents generally are compared to the ten-print database, and matches are recorded. Since there is uncertainty attached to these matches, probabilities are attached to each match. The advantage of these systems lies in their ability to perform high-speed searches of large databases.

Law enforcement officials embraced the new breakthrough, claiming that "AFIS technology finally has brought the use of fingerprint evidence into the twentieth century and promises to spur clearance rates more than any other single law enforcement tool" (Wilson and Woodard 1987: 1). To some extent the systems of the early 1980's did deliver by solving some crimes that would have remained open. Yet some applications were deemed less than successful, partly because police administrators failed to upgrade crime lab technicians and partly because of the failure to establish new policy and procedures that would extend the system from the crime scene to the courtroom (Moses 1987). Additionally, the system was not foolproof. Sometimes its output contained such a large number of likely suspects that it became more of a disincentive to the investigator and required the establishment of policies. For example, the department might specify that only the top three matches be included in an investigation of suspects, except for homicides, when all matches are investigated regardless of probability. Because partials often are of poor quality, some matches cannot be made unless (or until) the identity of a suspect can be put in AFIS along with the print. Despite these limitations and the costs associated with conversion, these systems allow police departments to search and identify thousands, even millions, of file prints with few labor-intensive costs (Fitzpatrick 1988).

The uncertainty that attaches to an AFIS match does not plague DNA matching, which, when it occurs, is with virtual certainty. (Most matches are stated as having an error rate of less than one in a billion). DNA is a genetic material found in many parts of the human body, including hair, blood, and other bodily fluids. Because DNA patterns are unique to an individual (unless they are identical twins), they provide the police and prosecutor with an irrefutable identification (Gladwell 1988). The National Institute of Justice reports that DNA kits are expected to be accessible to police crime laboratories throughout the United States before 1990 (Meese 1988). At the end of 1988, the FBI instituted a training course for state lab technicians in DNA matching protocols and procedures.

With over 80,000 rapes and 20,000 homicides per year and other identification methods being either inadequate or nonexistent, DNA matching systems may prove to be the greatest identification system available for crimes where physical evidence of sufficient quantity and quality is found (Gladwell 1988). Before it becomes universally accepted, however, the users and society will have to reconcile some ethical and constitutional issues concerning privacy and the invasion thereof. Proposals to build DNA banks already are encountering this criticism.

A different type of matching system is encountered in the softer sciences of psychology and human behavior. These are the systems that match on behavioral fingerprints. They include the progenitor, PATRIC, and more recent systems such as the FBI's Violent Criminal Apprehension Program (VICAP) and BCPD expert system for residential burglaries.

PATRIC basically matched crime incidents by the M.O. of the offender and recorded the number of "hits." The higher the number, the more likely the offense was committed by the same person. PATRIC differs from expert systems because it lacks the power to make inferences about the observed crime information.

VICAP uses pattern analysis to monitor case activity in the hope that it will eventually trace the travels of violent serial criminals across the United States. It stores information on unsolved homicides sent to the National Center for the Analysis of Violent Crime (NCAVC). For each new case entered, the system simultaneously compares and contrasts over one hundred selected M.O. categories of that case with all other cases stored in the data bank. The output is a listing of the ten cases in the violent crime data bank that most resemble the new case (Cameron 1988).

In addition to these activities, the FBI is developing an Arson Information Management System (AIMS) that "analyzes crime patterns to predict the times, dates and locations of future incidents, as well as the most probable residence of suspects" (Icove 1986: 3).

The FBI has had a long-standing interest in the use of expert systems to help unravel unsolved crimes and was the first federal agency to tap the power of these systems for law enforcement purposes. William Tafoya, a noted futurist at the NCAVC of the FBI Academy at Quantico, Virginia, has been a strong supporter of the application of these systems to solving crime (Cameron 1988). In line with this interest, the Behavioral Science Unit at the academy has developed an expert system that performs criminal investigative analysis of violent criminals (Tafoya 1987). It constructs a criminal personality profile of individuals based on reports from the crime scene, written media accounts, VICAP crime reports, violent crime research findings, and crime pattern analysis.

This type of profiling identifies the major personality and behavioral characteristics of an individual who has committed a homicide or other crime through detailed and painstaking analysis of the crime scene. The rationale for this process is that behavior reflects personality (Reboussin 1988). The primary inputs to the profiling process are information about the victim, the crime scene, and the behavior of the offender and victim. The primary output of the process is a description of the person who committed the crime.

The FBI's experience in developing expert systems for profiling offenders has led it to some conclusions of interest. It does not believe that the system will ever replace skilled profilers; rather it expects it to act as a profiler's assistant or consultant. The system can be a training aid to apprentice profilers, who could compare their own results with those of the system. (This same benefit could accrue to expert profilers also.) The comparison of results may invoke consideration of new variables and may lead to improvements to the system. Finally, it may allow profilers to spend less time on some aspects of the crime and more on others (Reboussin 1988).

Only two applications of expert systems at the local level have been publicized. The first is a rapist profiling program developed to show the ease of using VP-Expert, an expert system shell, for this type of profiling with the intent of encouraging other applications. The system however is small at least in terms of its limited number of rules (Cameron 1988). The expert system developed for the BCPD with National Institute of Justice support (Jacoby et al. 1988) and subsequently redeveloped for three other police departments (Tucson, Arizona; Rochester, New York; and Charlotte, North Carolina) with Bureau of Justice Assistance funds is more extensive. This system traces its roots to the Devon and Cornwall Constabulary in Exeter, England, where, under the initial direction and supervision of J. Brian Morgan, deputy chief constable, John Hulbert, chief superintendent, David W. B. Webb, superintendent, and it is one component of the force's comprehensive crime program plan.

The BCPD's expert system is substantively different from the federal efforts since it involves both matching and profiling from a large database of residential burglaries. The expert system stores information about residential burglaries that detectives and others use in investigating these crimes. Each piece of information--data on the environment, the type of entry, the extent and type of search, the property taken or not taken, and the behavior of the offender at the scene--relates directly to some inference detectives make when they investigate crime scenes.

The database contains closed and open case information. (In Baltimore County this totals about 3,800 cases.) When a burglary occurs, the crime scene information is entered into the computer, which develops a profile of the burglar. This profile and other elements of the current crime are compared to the database. A list of likely suspects is produced along with a similarity scale associated with each suspect. If no suspects meet the scale threshold set by the detective, the computer produces only the profile of the offender. Additionally, the system can calculate the similarity scale for a solved case against other unsolved cases with the intent of assigning responsibility to an apprehended offender during interrogation. Finally, by comparing unsolved cases to other unsolved cases, patterns of the type usually of interest to crime analysis units can be developed.

The system has been called a detective's assistant. It retains the best knowledge of the best detectives long after they have been promoted, retired, or left the department. As such, it has value for training newly appointed investigators, providing refresher courses for experts, and reducing some of the "paper chase" activities of investigators by shifting them to less skilled (less expensive) personnel. For example, fingerprint technicians can match the expert systems suspect's prints to partials taken at the scene, or the clerk maintaining stolen property lists can match the suspect's name to pawn shop lists.

The future of these systems looks bright. According to the Office of Technology Assessment (U.S. Congress 1986), sixteen agencies are currently using some form of computer profiling for law enforcement purposes. Their existence however, raises some troublesome issues.

Profiling can take two forms. The first is the identification of the individual associated with a specific event (such as a burglary) or the identification of the special traits of an individual that relate to a special act (such as violent murders). These profiles are designed to be as specific as possible to an individual. The second form of profiling is the troublesome one. This occurs when the profile turns into a stereotype for describing some group involved in illegal behavior. For example, a young, Hispanic male, carrying no luggage and paying for his airplane ticket with cash, is profiled as a likely drug courier. Persons fitting this description may be treated differently from all other passengers in the airport. As a consequence, it can be expected that the expansion of crime control profiling systems will bring right to privacy and due process to the forefront of debate. The "primary conflict is between the rights of the individuals selected (e.g. privacy, due process) and the purpose of the government in using computer profiles and their effectiveness in achieving that purpose" (U.S. Congress 1986: 88).

Equal protection arguments will inevitably be raised as expert systems move into local police departments. The Fourteenth Amendment clause prevents state and local police agencies from denying citizens equal protection in the discharge of their law enforcement responsibilities. Thus, equal protection "may require that the criteria on which the profile is based be related to the behavior in question; otherwise the selected group may be arbitrarily burdened. Additionally, the government's program would need to be rationally related to achieving a legitimate purpose such as detecting fraud, waste, and abuse or apprehending drug smugglers" (U.S. Congress 1986: 91).

The constitutionality of expert system use in law enforcement rests with the courts. In order to deprive an individual of freedom of action, law enforcement officers must be able to show that specific and articulable facts justify the intrusion (*Terry v. Ohio*, 1968). Case law on profiling lacks consistency and clarity. The sophistication of the profile, the profiling instrument's ability to select suspects accurately, and the policy and guidelines surrounding the use of profiles are all key issues that will have to be addressed as expert systems begin to multiply in police departments (U.S. Congress 1986).

In addition to the profiling issue, there is also the question of how expert are the experts. Since the system simulates detective knowledge, experience, and expertise, it also has the ability to simulate stereotypes and incorrect inferences. Validation mechanisms must be built to surround the expert system's rule base and check whether the rules are correct, under what conditions, and with what degree of certainty. Two questions need to be asked constantly of the system's responses: (1) if the system identifies A as the likely suspect, is it correct? and, (2) if the system says it is not A, is it correct? For example, if the system identifies a suspect but an arrest was not made, a negative evaluation has to be given if the reason for the non-arrest was that someone else was arrested and the suspect had an alibi (e.g., he was in jail) or the rules were wrong. Similarly, if a suspect is arrested but not identified by the expert system as a likely candidate, a negative rating has to be given if the suspect was in the database but excluded because of the rules or incorrect probabilities. The need for validation is constant and paramount.

Finally, there is also an organizational impact that police chiefs should be sensitive to: a subtle shift of power that occurs within a line organization that could be destructive to the expert system and its use. Problems with upgrading crime lab technicians or criminal records personnel to process the input into AFIS have already been noted. They should be expected when implementing an automated system.

Expert systems reflect expert knowledge, and in the case of the residential burglary system, the knowledge is that of the detectives and investigators. This is a system specified by them for their use. As a result, rules and usage should be under the direction of the detectives. However this, in effect, violates the traditional form of management information systems (MIS) supervision, which lodges supervision and direction with higher-ranking personnel than the users. Expert systems place responsibility on the users (detectives) to set the priorities for change and upgrade. The captains and majors who inherit the operational system should be aware of this difference and establish procedures that will permit experts to direct and guide the system.

Implementing real-world expert systems with a low risk of failure requires giving attention to four principal areas: people, management, application concerns, and system design and creation. "Most potential problems affecting the successful implementation of new technology have to do with people" (D.L. Smith 1988: 51). Without their being adequately trained so they understand expert systems, development efforts may be wasted. As Smith says, and as was borne out by the Baltimore County experience, "You need to explain to people what expert systems are and what role they play in the overall program. You need to take the magic out of expert systems" (D.L. Smith 1988: 52).

Involvement in the process, knowing its powers and limitations, and learning about the environment it works with (whether dispatching or residential burglaries) are necessary for successful implementation. The reason that these requirements seem to differ from the traditional MIS system requirements is that expert systems deal with operational reality, not management reports. Therefore they are only as good as their operators and users.

Expert systems may not dramatically improve a police department's arrest or clearance rate, but they can have a significant and substantial impact on resource allocation, the comprehensive collection of relevant information, and training.

PERSONNEL MANAGEMENT AND TRAINING

The quality of a law enforcement agency can be measured by its personnel, their experience, and, their training. It is universally recognized that the retention of quality personnel is a major concern of police managers (McLaughlin and Bing 1987). Although police managers can design and implement policies to minimize the adverse effects of turnover, many departments are on the verge of losing their experienced personnel en masse. The influence of unions (Fyfe 1985) and the 20/50 benefit that allows police officers to receive 50 percent of their income after twenty years of service have seriously affected police departments to the extent that many stand to lose significant numbers of experienced officers in the next five years.

Police organizations, and any other public or private organization, cannot retain staff over time for many reasons: dissatisfaction with salary, promotion, job content, coworkers and supervision; age and tenure with young employees with fewer years of service leaving at faster rates than older employees; repetitiveness and job autonomy; employee involvement and commitment to the organization; and opportunity for alternative jobs (Porter and Steers 1973; Price 1977; Muchinsky and Tuttle 1979; Mobley 1982). A recent National Institute of Justice survey of the problems and needs of police chiefs reported that a lack of professional opportunity is the greatest impediment to retaining staff (Manili and Connors 1988). Nominal salary increases were cited as the second significant personnel retention problem. Staff burnout as well as the raiding of personnel by other agencies were also found to be a major hindrance for police managers.

Turnover is not inherently dysfunctional. Studies have found that carefully managed turnover can result in positive consequences for an organization if the right people remain and the marginal employees depart (Dalton and Todor 1979; Abelson and Baysinger 1981; Mobley 1982; Hollenback and Williams 1986). But this control is difficult when county boards permit the replacement of law enforcement personnel only *after* the departure of an experienced officer.

When a police department is staffed with inexperienced personnel, there is a greater likelihood that discretionary errors will result. Weak or marginal cases entering the system are costly to the department in both time and money. Other more intangible costs may result from the violation of constitutional rights or victim anger which can be exacerbated by prosecutorial or court dismissals due to inadequate evidence collection.

Training Programs

To mitigate these damaging effects, police departments have recognized the importance of training as a means of transferring knowledge and experience from the learned to the novice. Police training has been at the forefront of attention in law enforcement circles since the late 1960's (Baker and Meyer 1979). The 1970's brought even greater attention to the subject when police were criticized by the media for failures in law enforcement and continued increases in crime.

The National Advisory Commission on Criminal Justice Standards and Goals (1973) produced comprehensive documentation that addressed new training developments and made recommendations for change. Its findings underscored the fact that deficiencies in police training impede law enforcement's goals of providing efficient and effective police services to the public in an equitable and just fashion. The emphasis of this national report, however, was geared toward the training of new recruits, in-service training of patrol officers, and the training of personnel at the supervisory level. Little attention was paid to training for investigators and the effective management of crime solving (Chappell et al. 1983).

As police personnel recruitment expanded in the 1980's from the pool of military personnel and veterans to include college and university students, minority ethnic groups, and females, training programs faced new challenges. They especially had to become dynamic (Walker and Flammang 1980).

Partly in response to the need for better training, the contemporary police manager turned to CAI and CBT (Wilkenson and Chattin-Nichols 1985). CAI is "the instructional technique of placing a learner in an inter-active mode with a computer that has been pre-programmed with a specific sequence of learning activities" (Waldron et al. 1987: 87). CBT refers to instructional programs that are solely computer dependent (Waldron et al. 1987).

The best-known CAI system is PLATO, developed at the University of Illinois in the 1960's (Archambeault and Archambeault 1984) and since modified for criminal justice purposes. In a joint effort with the Police Training Institute at the university, other police instructional programs were adapted for juvenile justice, criminal law, and report writing (Walker and Flammang 1981). PLATO has also been used for firearms training through computer-assisted target analysis (Palumbo and Connor 1983).

Despite the growing acceptance of CAI in the criminal justice environment, scant attention has been paid to the costs and benefits of this instructional technology; only a few short-term research studies have been undertaken. In addition, hardware purchases that are incompatible with the software selected have been a source of frustration in some CAI programs (Archambeault and Archambeault 1984). Other disincentives to CAI use exist. The sophisticated technology can cause anxiety and antipathy in instructors until they understand the hardware and software that support it. Some commercial CAI programs are inadequate because there are few experts available for assistance (Chambers and Sprecher 1980; Archambeault and Archambeault 1984).

Still, some police managers and training administrators are moving cautiously toward CAI. This may be due, in part, because negligible evidence has been introduced to show the educational value and cost-effectiveness of these systems. The cost effectiveness of CAI depends on a comparison of alternative means of training instructions. Such evaluations have received scant attention in the literature.

Despite the uncertainty, the potential for CAI application in law enforcement is real. The basic core of instruction so prevalent in police academies, the on-the-job training that rookies receive from more experienced partners, and the refresher or more sophisticated training offered by state or federal agencies may not be the most effective way to transfer knowledge. In the future, expert systems may play a powerful role in this training arena and even beyond, to field operations if they are applied to the issues of legal training.

Legal Training and Case Attrition

Personnel are the most valuable asset in any police organization. Planning and developing police personnel training programs requires a consideration of four primary issues: the type of training program, the availability of funds for training, the frequency of training after selection, and the effectiveness of training as a means to improve performance on the job (Smith 1988). Within the framework of these four areas, legal training is an area where police stand to gain the greatest return on their investment. Legal training programs have a major operational goal of minimizing case attrition by teaching police officers how to overcome evidentiary insufficiencies that may lead to case attrition.

The negative effects of case attrition for the criminal justice system are extensive and thoroughly researched (Vera Institute 1977; McDonald 1982; Garofalo and Neuberger 1987), with some studies finding that as much as 50 percent of felony arrests conclude without a conviction (Brosi 1979; Boland et al. 1988). There are a number of contributors to case attrition. Lack of victim cooperation, prosecutorial policy (Jacoby 1980, 1982), the cost of prosecution, community interest (Miller 1969), the dynamics of the courtroom work group (Eisenstein and Jacob 1977), the nonbureaucratic orientation of lawyers and judges (Saari 1982; Feeley 1983), delay in criminal courts (Church 1978), and even the socio-economic environment created by university towns, military bases, and tourist areas affect the operation of the justice system and a prosecutor's ability to bring cases to adjudication (National Center for Prosecution Management 1974).

Inadequate police training and its consequence, namely the submission of legally insufficient cases also rank high on the list. The repercussions of inadequate legal training in policing are grave for the law enforcement community and for the criminal justice community as a whole. When time, funds, and personnel are squandered because a police officer failed to Mirandize a suspect properly, interagency tension rises, morale is lowered, victim frustrations increase, and ultimately public confidence in the criminal process is eroded. Bringing good cases unmarred by constitutional and evidentiary problems is an important aspect of the police function. Consequently, training the law enforcement officer about legal requirements for prosecution is an integral part of most police academy curricula (President's Commission on Law Enforcement and Administration of Justice 1967a).

Unfortunately, prosecutorial involvement in the training of police officers and in transmitting information about changes in law or court rule too often has been spotty and inadequate. This is substantiated by persistent prosecutorial criticisms of the quality of police reports, their timeliness, and their legal sufficiency. Improvements in this area should be given top priority to break the cycle of inadequate police reports based on inadequate knowledge about what the prosecutor needs. The ideal situation is to have the basic legal training provided in the academy extended into the field and even to the arrest review and booking activities, much as McDonald envisioned for Nashville, Tennessee (McDonald 1987).

There is little justification for problems to continue to exist in this area since the technology is available and experts have demonstrated their ability to conduct successful training programs for police officers. Police officers can prepare legally sufficient cases. No more telling argument can be made than to look to the English law enforcement agencies and officers who had the responsibility for prosecution, or the direction of prosecutions, until 1986 when an independent prosecution service was established (Rozenberg 1987). Similarly, at a different level is the experience of Massachusetts, which until the last days of the 1970's routinely used police to prosecute misdemeanor cases.

One way training can be accomplished is to capture the expertise of the prosecutors, incorporate it into an expert system module, and append it to a CAI system for police training. From this basic system, another system can be developed that transfers selective knowledge to officers in the field and sergeants at the booking desk who can access the system for advice and consultation. This environment would strengthen the present procedures where experienced officers teach the rookie about the evidentiary needs of the prosecutor and the operational realities of plea bargaining and dismissals.

Although this is the least-developed applications area for expert systems, its value has been recognized by some departments, and smaller, less costly efforts are being undertaken. Most notable is the San Bernardino County Sheriff's Training Center, which is examining how computer-based training can improve the legal and evidentiary knowledge of its trainees. The center has developed a prototype computer-based training tool that drills the law enforcement officer in the four principles necessary to comply with the Miranda doctrine (Pogoloff 1988). (The lesson content about the Miranda decision was developed by expert trainers in the San Bernardino Sheriff's Department.) Trainees use a keyboard to process through the course. Tutorials first review the four principles of Miranda. Computer-generated graphics with various scenarios follow. For example, one pictorial shows a "burglar exiting a home with a pillowcase full of stolen goods. Students must choose whether or not they think the evidence in each scene is admissible without prior reading of rights" (Pogoloff 1988: 56).

The idea of capturing the legal knowledge of the prosecutor and retaining it for law enforcement use is not unrealistic, but some of the assumptions implicit in this activity may not be acceptable to all departments. This type of legal training assumes that the department embraces the goals of prosecution and conviction, in addition to apprehension and clearance. Officers and the department should be willing to measure their performance in this area by a different standard: namely, whether the case was accepted by the prosecutor (Jacoby 1982; Crawford et al. 1988)--no mean feat in many departments. It also implies that operational procedures will have to be modified for patrol officers and that additional responsibility will be given to the arrest and review functions to ensure the legal sufficiency of the cases prior to submission to the prosecutor. This is not a stance universally acceptable to law enforcement agencies, although its validity is rarely questioned with respect to repeat offender or career criminal programs. Expert systems offer a potential for breaking the cycle of inadequate police reports based on inadequate knowledge about what the prosecutor needs. It is not mandatory that police be lawyers, but it is imperative that they be trained to understand the legal sufficiency requirements of the cases they make and to have a means to test whether these requirements have been satisfied.

RESOURCE IMPLICATIONS AND COSTS

With the exception of expert system applications in the areas of training and program design, the vast majority of expert systems can be designated as operational, in contrast to the more traditional management information systems. As such, their construction and use places a different type of demand on police resources. Expert systems perform different functions for different users than the more familiar data-processing systems, and as a result, the impact on law enforcement resources is different.

The BCPD's development effort is estimated to have involved 4,000 man-hours at an approximate cost of $45,000 (Jacoby et al. 1988). These estimates, however, derived from a log of all man-hours expended on the project from November 1986 to February 1988, are not representative of expenses that other jurisdictions would incur since these costs are primarily developmental. Transfer costs are estimated to be one-third to one-half less than the developmental costs. But the point being made, to echo Smith, is that the man-hours equal involvement in the process, and "involvement . . . helps avoid the NIH or Not-Invented-Here syndrome" (D.L. Smith 1988: 52).

These manhours are expended on database reconstruction, data collection, automation of the data collection forms, making the system operational through plans and procedures, report generation, and the integration of the system with other existing law enforcement activities. Also, training personnel and monitoring the operations will place extra demands on the resources of the department. Moreover, the demand on manpower resources will continue long after the system is up and running. The rules will need monitoring and refining, new reporting procedures may have to be instituted, and as the technology advances, it should be integrated into the system through updating procedures.

There are other costs associated with expert systems in addition to manpower. They are the ones associated with the system itself. Expert systems require large amounts of memory, although they can be ported down to microcomputers as they were in Baltimore County. The BCPD residential burglary system operates on a COMPAQ 386 with 10 megabytes of memory and 60 megabytes of hard disk. The cost for this configuration is about $9,000. Most expert systems utilize shells, or special software packages, because they reduce system creation time and allow the users to create or modify the systems with only minimal help from outside. These shells have large license fees. For example, the Goldworks LISP shell used in Baltimore County costs $5,000, with a maintenance contract of $800 annually. With the addition of training, supplies, and other system-associated costs, the residential burglary system is estimated to cost a jurisdiction about $15,000 to $30,000 with an annual maintenance cost of about $3,000 to $5,000. In one sense, the costs of expert systems, like most other computer costs, are low relative to the costs required by the mainframe computers of the 1970's, but they are still substantial, and a department should investigate both the personnel requirements and the system costs before embarking on the adoption, development, and utilization of expert systems.

Expert systems are no different from other projects in that they demand proper direction and adequate staffing. They need strong policy direction and support by the chief, tight management controls, and the ability to make staffing readjustments as the project moves from the beginning stages to operational status. The most fragile part of these systems can be found in their use. If they are not accessible, and therefore, not usable, they are not worth the effort.

3
APPLICATIONS IN EXPERT SYSTEMS

The world of advanced technology has found a receptive home in law enforcement. Systems developed for the military have applicability to police operations and management. In many respects, the two environments face similar problems in personnel management, resource allocation, command and control, and operations. Even the phrase war against crime is an apt reminder of the parallelism between the two institutions. As a result, law enforcement, representing one component of the criminal justice environment, has always been a leader in the application of new technology to persistent problems, at least when compared to other public agencies.

Expert systems represent another step in the application of advanced technology to local law enforcement operations. While such systems do not provide the final solution to many of these perennial problems, they do add a new tool to an existing arsenal. The potential power of these systems is extensive. Because they attempt to simulate human thought in carefully defined areas, they add a degree of flexibility to a number of applications that did not exist before.

In this chapter, we look at three diverse areas of policing where the introduction of expert systems is feasible and is likely to be successful. Two of these areas have already been targeted by newly developed systems. The application of expert systems to command and control helps the dispatcher in decision making under difficult circumstances. The residential burglary expert system demonstrates the viability of expert systems in solving crimes. Finally, the use of expert systems to improve the legal training of police suggests how the knowledge of expert prosecutors can be transferred to police with the goal of reducing case attrition.

COMMAND AND CONTROL: DECISION-MAKING IN ACTION

Over the years, the activity involving police command, control, and communication has become increasingly complex, due not only to increased crime and the resultant growth in the size of police forces but also the increased complexity of the mission of the police. The ability of police managers to deal with this complexity varies. Some forces have well-trained officers who have the experience and training to deploy resources effectively, in others, such talent may be in the early stages of development. As training and specialization increase in this area, a search for new ways to keep the activity under control begins. The result has been the development of a series of techniques and strategies designed to assist law enforcement agencies in the task of resource deployment and management.

Most notable to date are systems supporting CAD, mobile digital communications (MDC), automated vehicle monitoring (AVM), and 911 communications. Although their goals are laudable, not all of these advanced systems have been unanimously accepted, and where they have been adopted, expectations have not always been met (Colton et al. 1983; Moran and Layne 1988). Despite a variety of problems and difficulties, there is general agreement that such tools are needed.

Command and control is the essence of policing because it spotlights decision-making at the operational level. However, the issues and complexities addressed in the command and control area are not so much related to reducing response time or the optimum allocation of vehicles and people (Larson 1978; Colton et al. 1983), as they are aimed at making the best decision under varying conditions. Making decisions uniformly and consistently, independent of the experience of the decision-maker with whatever information is available is key.

Decisions are made by people who have a variety of alternative actions from which to choose. Probably more publicity has been given to breakdowns in the 911 or emergency medical dispatch service systems than they deserve, but these failures point out the basic problems encountered in ensuring uniform and consistent decision-making. When the decision-makers are many, their levels of experience unequal, and the choices carry with them life-or-death consequences, these breakdowns will occur. It is not difficult to imagine a group of dispatchers ranging from novice to experienced making very different decisions even given the same information and the circumstances.

The quality of the information directly affects the quality of the decisions made. All too often when deployment decisions have to be made, the information level may not meet the needs of the decision-maker, sometimes because it is not available; sometimes because it may be inaccurate. For example, operational scheduling models (Larson 1978) may attempt to optimize the scheduling of officers by shift, taking into account such scheduled events as vacations or court time, but they may fail if other known events such as rock concerts or football games are excluded from the optimization process.

Still, humans, in particular experts, can and do make good decisions with incomplete information. They infer missing data from other data and come to a conclusion that is probably right most of the time.

Information is not always easily obtained or maintained. Even the best of systems has to commit to continuous monitoring and maintenance of the information base if it is to be useful. The Las Vegas Metropolitan Police Department, for example, warns about the continuous commitment needed to maintain accurate telephone numbers and addresses and states emphatically, "A system that provides incorrect information is almost worse than no system at all" (Moran and Layne 1988: 29). This can also be a problem for 911 systems, in particular the enhanced version which allows the entry of information about an address by the police department.

In retrospect, it is not the decisions made by law enforcement officials that have changed but the volume and the different types of resources available to meet those needs. Increased volume and increased alternative responses introduces complexity into the decision-making process, increases the number of and specialization of decision-makers. It also creates a need to treat resources (people, equipment, and information) in different ways, and establishes a strong demand for uniformity and consistency in decision-making.

Time Dimensions of Command and Control

Not all decisions are emergencies, nor are all command and control decisions necessarily complex. By looking at the types of decisions which are required in the command and control area in terms of time, we can reduce the level of complexity and address those issues that affect each part of the time spectrum. Then we can address the use of expert systems as they relate to each components.

Command and control decisions take place along a continuum of time that can be divided into three parts. The top level can be described as long-term or strategic decision-making. The expert decision-maker is concerned with what resources should be added or developed to cope with a changing population, a changing service mix, or a changing service level. The decisions that must be made deal not only with staffing levels but, more important, with the capabilities of the police to meet those changing conditions.

The second level occurs in a shorter time frame--months and days--and can be described as tactical decision-making. The task is to deploy resources in the best possible way or to optimize the ability to respond to calls for service. (The resource mix of the force is not of major concern since within this short time frame it is essentially fixed.) Typical decisions concern identifying resources to be assigned to shifts; desired response times; desired backup levels; what actions to take in bad weather; when shifts should be extended into overtime status; what situations need air support, specialized units, or officers with specialized skills; and when plainclothesmen should be utilized.

The third level requires timely action and can be described as real-time, operational decision-making. These are the demands for service that stem from 911 calls, the receipt of a silent alarm, or field patrol calls to the dispatcher. The decision to commit resources depends on the information provided by the callmaker and the training and experience of the supervisor or dispatcher. There may be substantial differences in the expertise of these individuals, and the quality of the decisions may reflect this situation. The decisions confronting the operational officer are varied, as are the data required for a competent decision. The information required to handle an automobile accident with personal injuries is quite different from that needed for a residential burglary. Similarly, the response to a burglary in progress is quite different from one reported to have occurred at least two weeks earlier. The dispatcher has to decide whether to dispatch at all, and if so, when and with what resources--police cars, ambulance, helicopter, interpreter, and so forth.

In the ideal world, the strategic planning undertaken at the highest policy level has been translated into a tactical plan that is made operational at the beginning and through the course of every shift at every precinct. The forces will have been scheduled and assigned according to a plan developed by the tactical decision-makers that should accommodate most of the situations that will occur on that particular shift. Daily operations then feed back into the tactical plans, causing short-run changes in those plans; then those needs will ultimately flow upward for long-term consideration.

Role of Expert Systems

To see how expert systems can complement the techniques and tools available to law enforcement, it is first necessary to identify the limitations of the present technology.

Strategic planning is not simply recommending increasing staff levels; it has to address training, specialized programs, and the acquisition of new technologies such as automated fingerprint systems, CAD, mobile dispatch terminals, and even expert systems. Without expertise at this level, police departments can find themselves with a serious mismatch between resources and requests for service.

The knowledge required to build a system with strategic planning capability will be quite different and perhaps more complex than for the other two levels of decision-making; however, there will be more margin for error, and the press of time will be less. While no one has yet attempted to build an expert system to assist in strategic planning for police command and control, one planning system has been attempted in a narrower area. This is the career criminal/repeat offender expert system, which attempts to use the expertise of consultants in an expert system to design a plan for setting up these types of programs.

The vast majority of work has occurred at the tactical deployment level. There are, of course, well-known studies and experiments drawn from operations research that attempt to optimize the scheduling of officers and the deployment of patrol (Kelling et al. 1974; Larson 1978; Whitaker et al. 1982). The missing ingredient that an expert brings to this problem is the ability to treat police resources differentially. An expert will consider not only issues such as balancing work load but also the integration of specialized characteristics that apply to a subset of police officers, such as army experience as a demolitions officer or the ability to speak Spanish or Vietnamese. In other words, depending on the situation, the expert would deliver a different mix of personnel and technology than would be determined by a linear programming model. Uncertainty can also be handled more appropriately using the expert system methodology. In the final analysis, a blend of OR and AI techniques are probably required.

The role of the expert at the operational level is quite varied but primarily focuses on the decisions to respond or not, and with what resource. As units are committed, the rules by which subsequent calls for service may be handled may be altered. Low-priority calls that have been dispatched may have to be suspended in order to service higher-priority calls and still maintain adequate reserves. If reserves are committed from one area, units may have to be transferred in or alerted to play a reserve role to a different patrol area. In some cases the standard operating procedures call for the dispatch of three units but current commitments require a reduction to two. Properly employed expert systems may assist the call takers, dispatchers, and police resource managers in making these decisions.

Example

A typical request for service comes in to the 911 center. The call taker fills in a field on the CRT screen which briefly describes the nature of the event occurring. Based on a set of rules, an initial determination of the type of event is made by the CAD system (e.g., burglary, accident, alarm). The call taker may agree or override that initial decision. Depending on the event assigned, the expert system will cause the program to operate in different ways. If the event requires immediate attention, only the minimum information required for the dispatch operation will be collected before passing control to the dispatcher. The minimum data set may include only address or other location information, or it may require the call taker to ask certain other key questions before passing control to the dispatcher. For example, if the caller says that the house is being burglarized, the first question might be whether the burglar is in the house. If the answer is positive, a question about location might be forced. At that point, all control would be passed to the dispatcher. But if the response was negative, additional questions may be asked without the pressure of time. This information will allow the dispatch operation to respond with the appropriate action.

The difficult decision here is to balance the need to gather sufficient information to cross the threshold values for generating an appropriate response without unduly delaying the initiation of that judgment. The system, as currently designed, allows the dispatchers to specify the types of questions to be asked by the call taker, along with the level of priority for asking such questions. This allows the system to change dynamically as decisions are made.

The dispatcher receives the call in a prioritized dispatch queue containing the elapsed time since the call and the priority for handling. The dispatcher can review the call directly (that same call could be being modified with lower-priority data at the same time) or can call for its dispatch. When a call is retrieved for dispatch, it will have already been geo-coded for the appropriate response sector either by the system or the 911 information. The selection of the draft response is policy driven by the sector, the priority, and the typical units to be assigned.

The rules for choosing the response are of several types. The first consideration is the current situation in the sector involved. If there are available units within that sector and the rules for maintaining a certain level of availability are not exceeded, the system will probably recommend dispatch. If there are no units available but a unit is handling a lower-priority call, that dispatch may be suspended in order to handle the new call. If there are no units available with low-priority dispatches and the call is of a high enough priority, a car from another sector assigned for backup of the affected sector may be utilized. The selection may also be affected by the time remaining in the shift. A car might not be dispatched on a low-priority call with an expected time to completion of two hours if the shift ends in thirty minutes. Similar factors would affect the choice of between two equally available cars. While a car might be technically available, the unit may be scheduled for a court appearance within the period of time required to complete a given call.

The dispatcher is presented with a recommended course of action that can be accepted or overridden. If the decision is in conflict with some policy or other fact known to the system, the dispatcher will be warned. If other actions should be taken (e.g., retain units on overtime status until the system returns to normal or change sector assignments), the dispatcher will be notified.

It should be clear that the decisions that a dispatcher makes cannot be made without reference to short-run tactical deployment and long-term strategic planning considerations. The expert system must incorporate these levels of knowledge as well. Herein lies the true value of an expert system in this aspect of command and control. All dispatchers are not created equal, and at times of peak activity, it would be easy for a dispatcher to forget these higher levels of consideration.

Conclusion

Expert systems clearly have a role to play in command and control. They will have more utility in forces that are faced with complex service delivery systems and rapidly changing environments. An expert system can also assist as a training tool and as a backup against the loss of a key employee who is in charge of strategic and tactical resource deployment. In either case, such systems should be viewed as one more tool that can be applied in efforts to serve the public interest.

SOLVING CRIMES: THE CASE AGAINST RESIDENTIAL BURGLARIES

An Old Story

It was a typical call--a distraught woman reporting a crime. Someone had broken into her house and stolen everything--her TV, VCR, camera, jewelry, cash, everything. Drawers were dumped out, and it looked as if the house had been ransacked.

In questioning her carefully, the dispatcher found out that the woman did not know when the burglary had happened; she had been at work all day. But the kitchen window was broken and the side door was open when she came home. The dispatcher promised a patrol car within the hour and asked her not to touch anything.

Patrol called the crime lab technicians, whose van arrived shortly after. They interviewed the woman, made a list of all the property stolen, including one unique piece of jewelry that could be identified, and examined the house for evidence and fingerprints. After the photos were taken and neighbors interviewed, the crime lab technicians filled out the incident report.

Within two days, the report was forwarded to the Crimes against Property unit where it was assigned to a detective and placed on the already sizable pile of cases for investigation.

This all-too-familiar scene is repeated daily in the United States more than 5,500 times. Burglaries are one of our most prevalent crimes. In 1987, 3.2 million burglaries took place, and two out of every three were residential (Uniform Crime Reports 1987). Next to larceny and theft, residential burglaries affect more citizens than any other offense, and burglars are the foremost invader of a person's privacy and space. They bring a sense of vulnerability and anger to thousands of persons who lead, and expect to lead, ordinary lives untouched by crime.

Burglaries are also one of the least solved of all crimes. Only 10 to 15 percent are ever solved (FBI Uniform Crime Reports 1987). Even rarer is the return of property to the owner if the burglar is arrested. Property is not, for the most part, easily identifiable and it can usually be disposed of quickly. If not fenced or given away, it is dumped in a creek, woods, or a city dumpster. In many cases, the owner may not even miss some items until long after the event. Fingerprints are rarely found at the crime scene, and when they are, the latents are more likely to be partial, of poor quality, and thus difficult to match even under the best of circumstances.

Too often, neighbors are poor witnesses assuming they saw the burglar. They are not trained to be suspicious or even to observe. Even in areas with neighborhood watch programs, the coverage of houses may be incomplete. Too many people work outside of the home, and too many think nothing is amiss even during a break-in.

This is not to say that burglaries are never solved. Many are. Sometimes the suspect is caught in the act; other times a detective can link a suspect to a name through street informants. With a name, it is quite possible that a fingerprint can place the suspect at the scene. Failing that, an investigation of known associates and friends may yield some property that can be identified by the home owner. Pawnshop records and stolen property files may yield important information or leads. An effective crime analysis or surveillance unit may be the key to an arrest. It is not unreasonable to assume that suspects leaving houses where drugs are sold will eventually need money to support their habits.

Solving burglaries places heavy demands on the detectives' workload. They can carry only a finite number of cases, which is one reason that the MCI concept has been adopted as an investigative classification tool. MCI solvability scores are computed for property crimes based on information collected at the preliminary investigation. The data assess the potential solvability of the case. If the scores are high enough, the case is worthy of further work and will be assigned to an investigator. If the potential solvability is low, the case probably will not be investigated. Although the MCI concept is accepted by the vast majority of law enforcement agencies, it has limitations. Because it is based on standards that can be measured by a set of objective factors, it cannot be very flexible and therefore cannot take into account individual variations in the nature of the cases. Nor does it take into account the prior experience and expertise of the detectives who may be influential in the solution of the case.

Critical to the solution is the experience and aptitude of the detectives. Knowing how to investigate a burglary and what inferences to draw from the crime scene comes from years of experience. Recognizing that some unusual circumstance may be the signature of a special burglar may produce an important shortcut to an arrest. This investigative ability and the storage of information is acquired over many years, but it can be lost in an instant through promotion or retirement. The knowledge and expertise of a twenty-year detective who retires is irrevocably gone; the newer detectives will rarely have access to it. This loss is felt by more than just the department. It extends even into the community as active offenders repeat their victimizations over and over.

Some New Hope

Law enforcement agencies have not given up hope in reducing this seemingly intractable problem. They have expanded the crime analysis function, integrated the information yielded from the streets with statistical tools for prediction, adopted automated fingerprint systems, developed stolen property files, and worked with the community to reduce opportunistic crimes through the installation of burglar alarms, dead bolt locks, and neighborhood watch groups. In this comprehensive plan, technology, procedures, and information are all brought to bear in the attack.

Expert systems provide another tool for solving crimes. They capture the best of the detectives' expertise in linking the events of the crime to the identification of the suspect through the behavioral fingerprint left by the burglar. This is accomplished by developing a knowledge base that makes inferences about crime scenes that lead to the identification of the suspect.

The traditional M.O. matching systems and crime analysis are based on two assumptions: that burglars are recidivists; and, that they tend to operate in the same way each time. Thus, M.O. systems matched data element to data element, pattern to pattern, and recommended detective action when the number of hits was high.

The weakness of these M.O. matching systems is not due to the assumptions used. Rather they are limited by the technology. The one-to-one correspondence of data element to data element did not give enough flexibility to the process. A particular burglar, for example, may normally use force to enter a premise, but if the front door is unlocked he may not have to. A front door may be the common entry point for another burglar, but he may use the back door or basement window if either is obscured. If large appliances were taken, the matching systems would not suggest interviewing witnesses who might have observed trucks at the premises. Neither would those systems produce a profile of the offender or suggest alternative lines of inquiry or recommend to discontinue the investigation.

When inferences are made about the connections between observed data and a likely suspect, it is done by humans, not machines. In part, this was due to the cost and complexity of the software and hardware. In fact, it was not until 1988 that the technology was available at affordable prices and was sophisticated enough to permit the construction of large-scale systems on microcomputers.

Expert systems can capture the thought process of detectives who make inferences about the suspect based on the crime scene. Essentially, they ask, "What does this fact or data mean to you?" If vise grips were used to gain entry, is this the mark of an amateur or a professional? If only one room was searched instead of the entire house and the room was the master bedroom, what does this say about the burglar? If a gun was left behind when it could have been taken or graffiti were smeared on the kitchen wall, what type of person would do this?

Experienced detectives make these inferences each time they view a crime scene or read a burglary report. The expert system frequently represents this knowledge in the form of rules. For example, if the alarm is cut, sterling silver is taken, and silverplate is left behind, the suspect is a professional. If the burglary occurred in a suburban area, the offender used an automobile or lived in the neighborhood. If food was taken and consumed, the suspect is either a vagrant or a juvenile. Conclusions can be drawn from individual or complex combinations of characteristics of a burglary. Included in these data are the environment, type of entry, method and extent of search, property taken and not taken, behavior at the scene, and others. These are the observed data used by the detectives and the primary input for the expert system.

Expert systems are case-based systems; their focus is the individual case and the goal is the identification of a set of likely suspects. Their narrow focus is, and should be, supplemented by the crime analysis findings. Crime analysis fits the individual case into the wider universe of trends and patterns. The focus of a crime analysis unit is the statistical description of crimes--by geographic area, over time, by types of crimes, by relationships to other crimes, and by changes. One can think of crime analysis as providing the picture of crime points in an environment and the expert system as the identifier of a suspect at one of these points in this picture. The two functions are complementary.

Information about closed and unclosed cases is collected to create a database for the system. This requires the department to tie incident report information to the identification number of the arrestee. Systems cannot be easily developed without this linkage. Each incident report is examined by the system. All possible inferences are made on the case data. Its characteristics, both observed and inferred, are then used in examining cases closed by arrest, and a list of likely suspects is produced. Associated with each name is a similarity scale that permits the ranking of a set of potential suspects. Even if no suspects are found, the system has provided a profile based on the inferred characteristics of the suspect. For example, a profile might be of an experienced, professional burglar who takes antiques and other valuables and works with accomplices.

Taking the identification as a lead, the detective or an assistant can first do a paper chase to determine whether latents or partials were found that could be the suspect's, whether stolen property might be identifiable and listed through pawnshop records, and who are the known associates of the suspect and whether any could provide information. If the paper chase produces any leads, the detective can move to the street. If an arrest is made, a search can be done to determine a likely set of unsolved crimes that this offender should be asked about for possible clearance.

The advantages of using expert systems to solve crimes have been implied throughout this discussion. Such systems:

* Retain the knowledge and expertise of experienced detectives long after they have left the unit.
* Will never forget a suspect even while he is serving time; and they will remember him if and when he returns to an active criminal life.
* Search records and match each to the incident faster than any human (in BCPD, 3,800 records are searched and matched in ninety seconds).

* Permit the comprehensive and uniform collection of information by the crime lab technicians about the crime scene.
* Are portable to the detective level; it is their computer, in their office space.
* Provide a basis for training investigators since they contain the best knowledge and best experience of the experts.

Conclusion

It is not difficult to envision the day when the expert system is linked to patrol officers through laptop computers or mobile dispatch terminals. By capturing the information at the scene and on-line utilizing intelligent prompts, time spent on report writing will be reduced. In addition, the collection of the information needed by the detectives will be comprehensive and uniform and delivered to them in a timely manner. These are not small achievements in a law enforcement agency. In moving toward the paperless society that patrol so eagerly embraces, the expert system may play a significant role.

LEGAL TRAINING OF POLICE

The CAD system dispatches a car to a burglary scene. The crime lab is called, and the information gathered by the technicians feeds into the residential burglary expert system, the automated fingerprint file, and the stolen property file. An arrest is made, but the case is dismissed in court because the chain of evidence was broken.

A persistent problem that plagues law enforcement agencies is training police officers and supervisors in the legal requirements for successful case prosecutions. The need affects all levels of policing--from basic training for new recruits, to refresher courses for experienced detectives. In addition, training and operations must incorporate changes in the latest court rules or legislation.

On the surface, training appears to be a simple function. It involves no more than the dissemination of information to students through lectures, manuals, and perhaps visual aids. Unfortunately, it is not quite so simple when dealing with the legal aspects of prosecution. First, the subject matter is complex and is constantly changing. Second, police are not specifically trained to deal with the type of information that is the purview of attorneys. Third, the training itself must be selective to avoid overwhelming the non-legally trained student. Finally, the actual implementation of the law may differ from what can be learned from reading statutes. The result is that the knowledge imparted by training programs may bear little resemblance to that needed by police officers to make operational decisions and by the prosecutor to prosecute.

The basic legal elements required to make a case do not change rapidly. The legal sufficiency of the case is usually defined by its three components: the elements of the crime, the constitutional requirements imposed on the apprehension, and the strength of the evidence, both physical and testimonial. Arrests, for example, are not sufficient if the arrestee cannot be placed at the scene of the crime. Recovered stolen property, narcotics, or guns are inadmissible as evidence if the chain of evidence has been broken by poor police handling and logging procedures. Even the testimony of witnesses may be damaged if improper lineups were conducted. These are only a few of the breakdowns that are far too prevalent. Most troublesome are the constitutional issues, since they tend to be more complex and variable in nature. Improper searches, Mirandas not given in a timely fashion, poor lineups, and non-approved wiretaps may taint cases to such a degree that dismissals are inevitable. Superimposed on this area is the changing complexity of the law and its requirements--asset seizure and forfeitures being a good case in point.

The basic training given police officers in the academy, and later through in-service training or even roll call, does not guarantee that the information they possess is up to date, accurate, or complete. What is needed is a means of keeping this type of information flowing from the prosecutor to the police agencies. There are a number of ways to accomplish this, and many are improved by modern technology. For example, videotapes explaining new court rulings or legislation and discussions about their impact on policing and subsequent prosecutions are useful. A comprehensive version can be utilized for training courses, and a shorter version can be available for roll calls. Although the problems of keeping the force up to date are enduring, they are not unsolvable. In the ideal world, every police officer should be aware of the legal implication of his or her actions, and have access to legal knowledge as it is needed.

For the vast majority of criminal arrests, those involving larceny or bad checks, for instance, preparing legally sufficient cases is routine. But there exists another universe not so routine, where cases are more likely to fail the tests for legal sufficiency.

A striking example can be found in narcotics investigations that involve surveillance, sting operations, or wiretaps. They encompass more complex evidentiary issues that must be satisfied if successful prosecutions are to be obtained. Some jurisdictions turn to the prosecutor for help when these cases surface, and if they are serious or important enough, a prosecutor may even be assigned to assist the police to ensure evidentiary sufficiency. But these resources are finite so other means of assistance need to be developed to fill the gap. One such tool is an expert system for legal advice that would be available for routine use by patrol and the sergeants who bear the responsibility for reviewing arrests.

Patrol sees a car weaving down the street exceeding the speed limit. The registration is checked; the car is not stolen. They stop it, and are suspicious that drugs are being transported, but a search of the trunk is necessary. Do they search, or do they need a warrant? A check with the legal expert indicates the need for a warrant and lists the elements of the crime that have to be reported before a warrant can be approved and issued. This information is used to produce the request for a search warrant.

In another example, the narcotics squad has brought in three suspects in a cocaine sales and distribution bust. The booking sergeant enters the details of the case into the expert system. After a few queries, the legal adviser pronounces the case approved for transmittal to the prosecutor. If problems are identified, the sergeant may be able to address them at an early stage.

The use of expert systems as legal advisers has multiple applications since they transfer the knowledge of the prosecutor to law enforcement personnel. Thus, they have value for training at academies for new officers and detectives, transmitting up-to-date information to the officers when the law changes, answering questions in the field as part of operations, and reviewing the sufficiency of the case for transmittal to the prosecutor. The ultimate goal is, of course, to present a legally acceptable case to the prosecutor and reduce case loss that can be attributed to police performance.

For each of the activities, different sets of information are utilized. Training academies require basic information for two purposes: to educate the new officers about the legal-evidentiary issues surrounding police actions (e.g., chain of evidence, Miranda warnings, lineups, search and seizures); and to make them aware of the objectives and needs of the prosecutor with regard to the evidentiary strength of cases by providing them with knowledge about the legal elements of a case. This stretches the concept of job performance to include whether cases meet prosecutorial needs. Training courses for investigators and detectives differ from the basic courses by focusing on the more sophisticated legal aspects of cases, especially with regard to strategies that can be used for apprehension, such as surveillance, wiretaps, stings, and reverse stings.

Up-to-date information about the implications of new laws or court rulings generally is transmitted by memo prepared by the prosecutor, the legal adviser to the police department, or an attorney in the force who can interpret the rulings and case law. As with most other written documents of this sort, there are problems with dissemination of information to the field. Thus, new forms of transmittal have emerged, notably the use of videos, which can be shown at roll call in two to five minutes.

In the field, there is another dimension of the problem facing expert systems: the transmission of information that has to consider *response time*, the *quantity* and the *quality* of information provided. Not only is fast response time a factor, but also the information provided must be succinct and relevant to the question. One cannot assume that patrol knows which procedures should be followed in all circumstances or has access to, or time to access, a manual that explains them. Instead, officers ask sergeants, detectives query partners, and sometimes, if the problem is difficult enough and relations are good enough, police ask prosecutors. With the exception, perhaps, of the last category, none of these activities guarantees receiving the right information or the right amount of information at the right time.

Operational systems need the ability to retrieve knowledge selectively. We have all thumbed through indexes looking for a word or topic that will refer us to the location of an answer to a question. If we are lucky, we have chosen the right word, can find the right pages, and quickly get a satisfactory response. Unfortunately, most of us know all too well the frustrations that can result from this apparently simple exercise when we cannot think of the right word.

Using an expert system augmented with hyper-text, to find the right words should pose few problems, and getting a response should be accomplished in a matter of seconds. Furthermore, much like a CAD system, the system should provide the opportunity to probe for more detailed information if necessary. For example, a police officer sits in the patrol car outside a house after responding to a domestic relations call--his first one. Quickly he queries his lap computer: "help-domestic." Instantly he is given the instructions, "Remove and separate, no force. Enter name and location address." He enters the address. The computer processes the data and responds that three prior calls for service in the past six months have been recorded for this premise. One involved violence and weapons. The officer radios for backup.

Prosecution is based on the written word. Each incident and arrest report must contain enough information to enable the prosecutor to determine the legal sufficiency of the case, file the appropriate charge, and avoid having to request additional investigation. One responsibility of the arrest or booking sergeants or officers is to identify inadequate or insufficient cases and order corrections, where possible, or direct the prosecutor's attention to potential problems if necessary. Properly designed expert systems can be developed to assist this process in two basic ways: by establishing an automated checklist of information or activities that should be performed in areas with a history of being troublesome, and by establishing the criteria needed by the prosecutor for certain cases.

Not all activities conducted by the police have such problems, but some do, and those are the ones that need to be addressed by the system based on the experiences of the police and the prosecutor. A good example is the assistance that can be provided to police in the development of requests for search warrants. The information requirements for the different situations can be specified and then retrieved as needed. This procedure does not need an expert system to support it; however, it can be part of the overall system within which an expert system is imbedded.

The expert system is useful in reviewing search warrants because various cases call for different applications and assessments about adequacy or completeness. For example, the evidentiary requirements for cocaine busts conducted with a wiretap and search warrants are more complicated than those of a street arrest for simple possession. The expert system can make the decisions about what is needed and whether the responses are satisfactory for the prosecutor or whether additional investigation is required. All of this can be accomplished on a routine basis because the knowledge of the prosecutor is incorporated into the system. Case attrition because of inadequate police work or reports should be greatly reduced with the availability of legal expert advisers.

The cycle is completed when the officer makes the proper decisions based on adequate knowledge, follows the

procedures correctly in making an apprehension, and files a
report that allows the prosecutor to determine whether the case
is legally sufficient.

Conclusion

Training extends far beyond the academy and should be
integrated with the subsequent activities that police and
prosecutors perform. One tool for integrating training activities
with operations and report writing can be found in expert
system technology. The real difficulty will be in constructing the
knowledge base to capture the variations in events e.g. searches,
seizures of property or surveillance.

Laptop computers can be programmed to provide
intelligent checklists for police officers at the crime scene. Such
checklists would not be uniform but would dynamically change
as additional information is entered and the system determines
the true nature of the event. This will enable them to collect the
proper elements of the offense and arrest that are needed by the
prosecutor to judge the merits of the case. Booking sergeants
can access the prosecutor's information needs for specific
situations and the laws that relate to them. With this advantage,
the entire criminal justice process benefits. Some of these
benefits return to the department. For now, it is possible to add
other aspects of performance into the police personnel system.

The cost of these innovations is not high when compared
to the flexibility and responsiveness that the new technology
brings with it. By capturing the best of prosecution and
translating it into police training, operations, and report writing,
many of the troublesome areas are smoothed. The dynamics are
such that these systems can be updated, expanded, and adjusted
to the real world of policing and prosecution. More important,
accurate information is being disseminated in a uniform and
consistent manner to all who need it when they need it.

4

BUILDING AN EXPERT SYSTEM

The process of building an expert system is generally thought of as a five-stage process: problem identification, conceptualization, building the knowledge base, selecting implementation strategies, and validation and modification. At each stage, the potential for making a decision or ignoring a problem that would cause the expert system to fail is present. Therefore, each has to be approached carefully and conducted prudently.

Problem identification is crucial because not all problems are suited to the development of an expert system. The selection of an inappropriate subject may guarantee failure. If the topic is suitable for development, the conceptualization stage follows. Here, a comprehensive framework within which the expert operates is developed so that as many aspects of the problem as possible are understood and included. It is at this stage where the boundaries of the problem must be clearly delineated.

With the framework in hand, the next step is to build the knowledge base. The knowledge base contains facts, information about how to use the facts that are known about the event or situation the expert system is addressing, and even knowledge about knowledge. Ultimately facts from the database are used with knowledge to reach conclusions about data not currently known or to advise the user as to some conclusion. A variety of knowledge acquisition techniques are available to aid in the construction of the knowledge base, and one will have to be selected. The knowledge engineering phase will focus on decisions about how knowledge will be represented and what search methods are most efficient for the problem under consideration. These decisions will define the required database and influence the implementation strategy.

The implementation strategy is constrained in part by the requirements of the knowledge engineer and in part by the needs of the user. Both factors are crucial in determining the delivery system and the manner in which the system will be integrated into the agency.

The final, and perhaps most important, part of the process (excluding problem selection) is testing, validation, and eventually modification. The long-term utility of the system will depend in large measure on its credibility and its adaptability to changing environments.

Each stage of this process has unique problems that must be addressed in order to maximize the likelihood of completing the project successfully. Although the principles should hold across a wide spectrum of law enforcement and other applications of expert systems, the examples used in this discussion relate to the BCPD's residential burglary, Delaware's CAD, and the career criminal-repeat offender expert systems.

PROBLEM IDENTIFICATION

The most likely reason for the failure of an expert system project is that the problem selected was inappropriate. There are several generally agreed upon criteria that should be applied when considering the application of the expert system technology.

1. The problem must be of sufficient size that a person cannot routinely solve it in a few seconds, but it should not be so large that the human expert needs days to solve it.

2. There are experts available who are significantly better at performing the task than others who must do so.

3. The expert's knowledge can be expressed as a set of facts and rules, and those rules may have a degree of uncertainty.

4. There is reasonable probability of having a significant impact on the organization, and the cost of development and time frame of implementation are within reason. In other words, the problem is worth solving.

5. Users are interested; there is a good implementation environment.

Size

Problem size is an extremely important issue especially if it is the agency's first venture into the world of expert systems. If the problem chosen is trivial, the system will not be used and is not worth the effort. If a reasonable person presented with the appropriate information could quickly arrive at the proper conclusion, the problem is too small. If, on the other hand, an expert needs days to arrive at a conclusion given all the necessary data, the expert system is probably too complex to build. The "telephone test" is probably the most useful standard for determining relative complexity: can the expert explain his or her reasoning process over the telephone in less than an hour? If the problem fails this test, either discard the application or determine if the boundaries of the system can be drawn more narrowly eliminating some of the complexity.

Experts

The knowledge of experts is clearly mandatory, but their availability may be doubtful. If clearly superior individuals are available and capable of explaining the reasoning process by which they solve the problem, the search may be over. If the candidate expert is not able to communicate or articulate the problem-solving process or is either unwilling or disinterested in the project, the only solution is to find another expert.

There are also applications that require the knowledge of multiple experts. These are likely to occur when some of the knowledge required is universal or generic and other pieces of knowledge are local and/or unique. Any expert will have that subset of knowledge that is universally true, but he or she will also have some knowledge that is dependent on the location of the problem or the range of his or her experiences. This is particularly a problem when the system requires different rules for different geographic areas. Unique knowledge occurs when only one expert has observed the set of circumstances necessary to derive any conclusion about a particular event.

Depending on the circumstances, either single or multiple experts can be used effectively. Multiple experts were used in the burglary system largely because there was significant local knowledge, and no one detective had experience with all three regions of the county. A single expert dispatcher was used in the CAD system because she was the most experienced and the system was being applied only within the region of her knowledge. Several experts were used in the career criminal-repeat offender project in order to cover different aspects of the same problem because the application was designed to satisfy a variety of local criminal justice environments.

Rule Based

The expert systems being built today rely primarily on production rules, one of several different forms of knowledge representation. This requires that the knowledge used to solve the problem must be capable of being expressed in the typical if-then form of a rule. If the expert needs visual or auditory input, the problem is probably too complex for an expert system application. Further, if the rules do not contain some degree of uncertainty that can be expressed as true a certain percentage of the time ("if this, then that, 85 percent of the time"), the problem is probably better solved by a written protocol such as those found in the typical home family medical guide or standing operating procedures.

Even if one feels fairly confident that the key concepts used by the experts can be expressed as facts and rules, there is always a question of validity. Are they in fact true, or at least true with the appropriate certainties assigned? To what extent does there exist a global, recurring set of facts and rules derived in widely diverse environmental settings that apply everywhere and a local set that apply only to the specific jurisdiction? Experience indicates that this distinction is important for the residential burglary expert system and that the validation of the rules will occur during the course of system operation.

The knowledge base for a dispatcher can also be represented by production rules; however, it is much more likely to be dominated by local rules than global ones, in large measure because of the mix of events and the array of resources available to respond. Each will vary considerably across jurisdictions. The career criminal-repeat offender application is also amenable to formulation by production rules. The similarity in the adjudication process across most states ensures that a large portion of the rules will be global; however, the role that uncertainty plays in that set of rules is not at all clear.

Value

It is possible to build an expert system that satisfies the technical criteria for selection, that is constructed at an appropriate cost within a reasonable time frame and is seen as a failure in the agency. Failure may occur because the problem solved is not important to the mission of the organization. For that reason, it is best to pick from among the list of technically feasible problems those projects that can be developed in a reasonable period of time, at a reasonable cost, and with the highest measurable benefits for the resources required in the development. In other words, a small project with a high probability of success is preferable to a large project with a low probability of success.

The residential burglary system met these general criteria because it had multiple uses--as the detective's assistant, as a trainer, and as a departmental historian. There is no doubt that there will always be expert and nonexpert detectives operating in police departments for at least two reasons. First, the training received (if any) by newly appointed detectives is rudimentary and deals more with process and paperwork than crime-solving. Most of the knowledge is gained by on-the-job training and interaction with experienced detectives. Second, the rotation policy of most departments guarantees that the expertise of experienced detectives will be lost when they go to a new assignment.

In addition, there were other major benefits: solving the case more quickly and with fewer resources. With clearance rates for residential burglaries hovering in the 15 to 20 percent range, the potential for organizational impact is great. However, if the low clearance rates are due not to the lack of expertise but rather to the low inherent solvability of these cases, then the application of this technology may not improve clearance rates at all.

The Delaware CAD expert system was easier to justify since it is part of a much larger system that has its own intrinsic value, including geo-reference, complaint tracking, and car status. In fact, this particular strategy of embedding the expert system in a larger system is probably the model that many other systems will take in the future. Expert systems built as subsystems will still be prototyped on the smaller development platforms prior to installation.

The career criminal system is more typical of most current applications in that it is a stand-alone system--neither integrated into another set of operations nor embedded in a larger system. Since the scope of its use is national and the alternative costs are high (a high-priced technical assistance consultant), this application also satisfies the value criteria.

Finally, the timing and cost of development must be reasonable for a successful application. The residential burglary expert system has an estimated installation time of four months and an out-of-pocket cost of about $30,000 to $40,000. This cost includes hardware, software, and the construction of a local knowledge base. If the hardware is already available and the department does not want to add local rules to the "generic detective knowledge base," then these costs can be reduced to about $10,000. This does not include, however, in-kind contributions of the department. Examples of such costs are personnel utilized in knowledge acquisition sessions, retrospective reconstruction of cases of active burglars, and training. To justify these expenditures, in-kind and money, the potential benefits should clearly outweigh the costs.

Users

One sure way to ensure failure is to select an application where the ultimate users have little interest in the project. Even if the initial development is completed without difficulty, the validation and modification of the system is impossible without strong user support. The users of expert systems are more likely to be operational personnel rather than those in management or data processing. As a result, it is possible for the system to work even with lukewarm management support as long as the users recognize its utility.

The long-term utility of the residential burglary system, for example, will be determined by its use by detectives. This means that the system, in addition to its merits, will be evaluated by its ease of use, availability, location, and effectiveness. All of these issues depend on the way the system is integrated into the department and on the ability of the system to be validated and modified. The verdict on these issues is not likely to be in until at least a year of experience is available to evaluate the knowledge base and its engineering and stability.

CONCEPT DEVELOPMENT

There are two major actors in the development phase: a domain expert and a knowledge engineer. The domain expert, as the name implies, has knowledge about the domain of the application. This includes knowledge about the problem area and especially knowledge about the scope of the problem. For example, a national-level expert may not be useful in a largely local problem area such as CAD. Even if these criteria are met, the domain expert is unlikely to have been involved with the construction of an expert system. The knowledge engineer does not necessarily have to be familiar with the domain or the subject matter. His or her task is to take the knowledge from the expert and apply it to the construction of an expert system. A knowledge engineer who has domain experience is infinitely preferable (although unlikely). In this section, we will examine some of the difficulties with experts and some steps that are necessary prior to entering into the formal knowledge acquisition stage.

The primary role of the knowledge engineer is to work with the domain expert (e.g., detective, dispatcher, consultant) to draw out the key concepts and aspects of the expert's thinking process and to represent that knowledge in a way that is suitable to the computer-based expert system. This may seem to be a straightforward process, but it is not. As with any other area of human communication, the potential for misunderstanding is always present, and that potential increases significantly if the knowledge engineer has little or no experience in the expert's field. That, in turn, may affect the level of confidence that the expert has in the knowledge engineer.

In most cases, the experts do not consciously think through the process that they follow in reaching a conclusion about an event. Probably they do not even fully realize the range of inferential activities they undertake. Thus, the first task is to develop a conceptual model of the problem in order to help the experts organize their thinking process, help educate the knowledge engineer in the domain of the expert, and provide a road map for the entire knowledge acquisition process.

The goal of the conceptualization process is to produce at least three outcomes: a concept that illustrates the expert's global view of the problem and the boundaries thereof, that defines the required input data, and that specifies the expected outcomes of the expert's thought process.

One conceptual model of a burglary, for example, is based on the activities of the burglar that occur before the break-in, during the break-in, and after the break-in. In most cases, detectives can observe only the results beginning with the middle stage, although they may be able to make inferences about the other stages. For example, target selection and mode of transport to the scene, both of which occur prior to the break-in, may be just as important in the inference process as actual data on the property taken. The likely method of property disposition may be inferred from data on the scene as well. Both sets of inferred data may give a clue to the identity of the criminal.

Figure 4.1

FRAMEWORK FOR RESIDENTIAL BURGLARIES

* **Victim Characteristics**   * **Property Taken**

* **Environmental**   * **Property**
  Location   **Available, but not**
  Risk   **Taken**
  Temporal

                                      * **Behavior at**
* **Entry**   **Scene**
  Method and   Damage
  level of   Evidence
  sophistication

                                      * **Transportation**
* **Search**   **Used**
  Type
  Extent

                                      * **Suspect**
                                        Description, if
                                        Observed

Almost all residential burglaries can be described with the answer to several simple questions:

1. Why was this residence chosen?
2. How did the offender(s) enter?
3. What activities occurred in the residence?
4. What was taken?
5. How will the property be disposed of?

The answers to these questions lead, either directly or inferentially to a profile of the criminal. That mental picture includes the standard demographic profile--age, race, and sex--but also extends into other areas, such as competence as a burglar, use of accomplices, likely area of residence, means of transport, and personal habits (e.g., drug and alcohol use). These inferred data, coupled with observed data, can serve to narrow the focus of search quickly for the expert detective.

One's first inclination in building a system such as the burglary expert system is to jump right in and work with the existing, observable data and the more obvious knowledge that the experts have about behavior on the crime scene and the probable characteristics of the criminal given that behavior. This approach assumes, however, that all the relevant information for making inferences is already available, and it rarely allows for the development of a conceptual model, which then precludes having a framework to assist in successful knowledge acquisition.

If multiple experts are to be used, it is useful to develop the conceptual model with the principal expert and then to elicit comment on that model from several other experts. The views of all the experts must be synthesized and then a final version can be proposed. (See Figure 4.1)

In the residential burglary system, we found that the experts were trying to infer characteristics of the perpetrator by observing what had taken place at the crime scene. These characteristics are the primary outputs of the expert system. Experience showed that the most convenient way of thinking about a process was to assume the place of the burglar (at least as simulated by the expert) and build a model of his thought process--or lack thereof.

Developing a conceptual model of a dispatcher presents a somewhat different problem. The input data concern the nature of the incoming call, the current state of the resources under the dispatcher's control, the potential set of different responses that the dispatcher might choose from, and the policy guidelines and procedures that govern the use of resources under a wide variety of system resource utilization rates. The outcomes are the decisions to dispatch or not, the different resources to dispatch, and the redeployment actions required based on the new utilization rates. (See Figure 4.2)

In the same way that the model of the burglar suggests the types of data that must be collected at the scene to satisfy the needs of the expert, a model of the dispatch process suggests the data that must be collected by the call-taker in order for the dispatcher to arrive at the appropriate decision. This modeling process indicates that there are in fact two types of expertise required: to categorize the type of call properly and to ask the proper sequence of questions. The call-taker must be able to ask the right sequence of questions depending on the type of

Figure 4.2

COMPONENTS OF COMPUTER-AIDED DISPATCH

* **Type of Call**

* **Categorizes Calls**

* **Location of Cars**

* **Automates Call Processing and Dispatching Functions**

* **Provides Algorithmic Decision Support**

* **Automatically Times the Length of Calls**

* **Provides New Information Used for Management**

incoming call; for example, the pattern for an accident is quite different from that for a burglary in progress. This is an even more crucial issue if the call-taker must deal with medical information and symptoms.

The career criminal consultant system followed a slightly different path. The search was for a unifying theme that could tie the different components (police and prosecutor programs) together without distorting either program since the programs could exist for either or both parties and operate separately or in a cooperative fashion. The conceptual model that evolved was a linear systems model that identified the overall objective of the program--removing active repeat offenders from positions of threat to public safety, using whatever tools were available to the local jurisdiction, and separating those decisions under the control of the program planner from those that were not. For example, the prosecutor or program planner could choose an offender-based repeat offender program but could not select a prearrest model without police cooperation. The role of the expert was to identify the potential tools that were available to

Figure 4.3

COMPONENTS OF CAREER CRIMINAL/REPEAT OFFENDER

Internal To Program

* Type of Program
Pre-arrest
Post-arrest

*** Repeat Offender
Designation**
Before charging
At charging
After charging

*** Limits on Prosecutorial
Discretion**
Dismissals
Plea bargaining

*** Program Monitoring
and Management**

* Primary Decision-Maker
Police
Prosecutor
Both

* Program Organization
Unit
Integrated

*** Type of Case
Assignment**
Horizontal
Vertical
Team

*** Evaluation and
Modification**

External To Program

*** Inter-Agency
Coordination**

*** Probation and Parole
Structure**

* Legislative Environment
Habitual offender
acts
Sentencing guidelines
Mandatory
minimums

be applied and to develop a program plan that would allow those tools to be used within an environment of constraints.

Each of these examples show the difficulties of initiating a knowledge acquisition process without some framework within which the knowledge can be organized. Figure 4.3 shows the conceptual framework used in the design of the career criminal--

repeat offender expert system. It identifies the major areas where information is needed before a program plan can be developed. While there are some risks that enforcing a rigid model on the process, especially if it is the wrong one, will prove inhibiting, it is more probable that the lack of one will be chaotic. The knowledge acquisition process should feed back into the conceptual model by modifying and extending it. It also serves as a basis for the development of training courses.

BUILDING THE KNOWLEDGE BASE

Once the framework has been developed, it is time to begin the difficult task of knowledge acquisition, which will ultimately determine the credibility of the system. There are a variety of ways to acquire knowledge, including interviews, man-machine interaction, and induction. Each has problems and limitations. The knowledge engineer may be forced to innovate by modifying any particular approach or employing multiple methodologies. No matter which method is selected to build the knowledge base, much of the information acquired will be "inexact"; it may not always be true for all situations. All expert systems have to take this into account as part of building the knowledge base. Assigning certainty factors to the knowledge (rules in this case) is part of this process.

Knowledge Acquisition

Obtaining knowledge from an expert is difficult for a variety of reasons, not the least of which is that there are few clear rules on how to do it. Some techniques are intensive personal interviews, fully automated man-machine interaction, and induction from data.

In the classic method, the expert and the knowledge engineer sit down with pen and paper and perhaps a tape or video recorder. This interview process or debriefing typically concentrates on conclusions or decisions, the data used or observed in reaching a conclusion, and the reasoning process. If different conclusions are possible, the interviewer will want to know what information would have caused the expert to change that conclusion and to what alternative conclusion.

This procedure is time-consuming and depends inordinately on the ability of the interviewer to ask the right questions at the right time. From a methodological point of view, there are serious questions about the accuracy of the information that can be obtained using the interview technique.

Among the reservations are whether the knowledge engineer has a true understanding of the mental process of the expert and, whether the expert introduces myth into the explanation or attempts to dress up his or her reasoning. One cannot dismiss the classic problems of instrument reactivity and the Hawthorne effect--that the expert's responses are affected by the experiment. Still, until other methods become better developed, this technique will continue to be used.

The second method, man-machine interaction, depends on the successive differentiation between alternative conclusions and associated cases by asking the user to supply distinguishing traits. The software that supports this type of knowledge acquisition typically asks for a set of alternative conclusions, such as dispatch, dispatch later, or never dispatch. The users are supplied with examples of calls that resulted in each possible type of decision and are then asked to identify the characteristics that differentiate that call from a comparison set. This process continues until the system can build rules to differentiate the cases. In one sense, this process is similar to the actual interview process. It is different in that it is not necessarily concerned with the unobserved structure of the reasoning process, only the end result. Obviously the method is limited by the cases used. If they do not cover all distinctive conditions, some rules may not be included in the system. Additionally, they may exclude relatively infrequent situations that should be included in the knowledge acquisition process. This implies that statistically drawn samples of cases should not be used to this task unless they are highly stratified.

The third approach is that of induction where general conclusions are derived from specific raw data. Here an attempt is made to generate rules from the data by finding the set of variables that best separate the cases into the observed set of conclusions or decisions. For example, if the possible decisions are dispatch immediately, dispatch later, or do not dispatch and the data are priority of call, availability of cars in sector of call, and availability of cars in other sectors, then the observed cases could be classified by the level of each of those variables producing the actual outcome. The rules that were inferred may not even be in the reasoning process of the dispatcher, but the results are accurate. Obviously inductively generated rules, like any other, must be closely monitored.

The major drawback of the second and third methods is that users may reject these synthetically created rules even if they perform reasonably well. In the third case, users must be heavily involved in reviewing the outcomes of the induction research since they have less direct contact than with either the interview process or the man-machine dialogue. Probably more important is the question of selection bias introduced by the cases selected for review or the data selected for analysis. This is not the time to develop averages; it is the time to look for exceptions.

The residential burglary project produced some imaginative solutions to many of the problems associated with knowledge acquisition. Not only were multiple sites involved across the United States, but within each site there were local differences that demanded multiple experts. This effectively argued against one-on-one interviews between the experts and the knowledge engineer. Although each site collected the typical incident information, the majority of the data required by the expert system were not collected. This ruled out using an inductive approach based on raw data analysis. The solution was to tap a broad range of views in building the initial knowledge base by assigning the detectives and crime lab technicians to small focus groups. Each group was led by a detective experienced in burglary investigations and was facilitated by one or more researchers. In this way, the initial knowledge acquisition step was conducted independently with each group. The focus group technique has proved successful for single departments, and for identifying generic knowledge across departments.

The results produced rules, statements of "fact," and assertions about burglars. Each group's output was compared across groups, a comparison that yielded a subset of knowledge that was uniformly considered to be true, a subset that was in conflict, and a subset that was unique (unduplicated by any other group). The conflict set tended to break into two parts: that knowledge about which there was fundamental disagreement and that knowledge which was different because of external factors (such as local knowledge that could not be generalized). The final set, which contained unique rules and statements, could neither be confirmed nor denied. (See Figure 4.4)

To further validate the knowledge base, the rules and statements generated from the focus groups were evaluated by a larger group of detectives, who were asked to agree or disagree with the rule or statement on a scale ranging from strongly agree through strongly disagree. This review provided a check on the consensus of the focus groups and on the unique constructs (which could not be validated in the earlier process).

Figure 4.4

SELECTED RULES BY TYPE AND PROBABILITY

Type of Rules	*Percent Agreement*	
	Site 1	*Site 2*
* Uniformly Considered to be True		
If extensive vandalism, then not an adult.	65	67
If more than one entry point, then accomplices used.	62	82
If risk reduction precautions, then not an amateur.	83	92
If drugs or prescriptions taken, then an abuser of drugs.	100	100
* In Conflict		
If pry tool used, then sophistication not high.	55	85
If search was by ransack, then accomplices used.	35	80
* Unique to Jurisdiction		
If target in barrios, then suspect lives in barrios.	93	--
If entry by "doggie doors," then suspect juvenile.	62	--
If entry through "milk boxes," then suspect juvenile.	--	91

* MO Signatures

If "L" shape cut in screen at point of entry, then signature Ron Allen.

Additionally, this approach proved useful for validating rules during the early stages of porting the knowledge base from one jurisdiction to another.

Uncertainty

The knowledge acquired is represented by a series of production rules, which are generally inexact, that is, they cannot be stated with a certainty value of 1.0. As a result, each rule has associated with it a certainty factor that varies by the percentage of time it actually occurs. For example, a detective might observe a particular method of entry and infer from it that the burglar was a juvenile, however, there is also some possibility (although smaller) that it was an adult. Thus, the rule is assigned a certainty factor in the range 0 to 1. This is particularly important when the system draws conclusions from inferred data. In that case, the system must include not only the certainty associated with the current inference but also certainties associated with any input data.

It is important to differentiate between certainty factors and other methods of expressing certainty. Certainty factors as used here assign a value without being bound by the mathematical rules governing Bayesian probabilities. Some expert systems use Bayesian probabilities, others use certainty factors, and still others use fuzzy logic as a method of handling uncertainty. For now it is enough to know that some method must be used and that there is more than one.

There are several ways to assign certainty factors to rules. The best method is to derive them from real data, although this may not be possible in the early stages of development. Nevertheless, it amplifies the need for building an evaluation process to correct the certainties as data become available. Another technique for assigning initial certainties uses the subjective assessment of the expert. Still another alternative is to base them on the percentage of disagreement recorded from the rule or statement evaluation instruments. All three methods appear to be usable, although a formal evaluation will have to wait until more accurate certainties can be derived. Some of the rules that were derived may be myths although they are widely held to be true. This also suggests the need to review the data continually and challenge "new experts" for new rules as environmental, economic, or demographic factors change. There is also the possibility of having the system itself suggest new rules based on induction. Such rules, however, would have to be evaluated by the experts, and they should fit into the conceptual model or should suggest changes to the that model. That requirement identifies one of the differences between predictive statistical models and logic-based expert systems.

Finally, the knowledge engineer must be on the lookout for meta-rules, or rules about rules. Consideration should be given to isolating sets of rules if they apply in only limited circumstances. Meta-rules can be developed that control whether that isolated set of rules should be considered.

IMPLEMENTATION

After the initial specification of the knowledge base and the supporting database, the next step in the process is building the delivery system. This encompasses choosing the software that best applies to the problem being addressed by the expert system and to the technical capabilities of the users; selecting the appropriate hardware for the department and the users or adapting the system to run on available computers; and integrating the system into the organization. The various combinations that can be produced by these three areas complicate the task of providing a delivery system. Each decision has to be made in the light of the other delivery components.

For all the importance and consideration given to the delivery system decisions, the final selections should rest on one criterion: can the delivery method produce an end-product that will satisfy the intended users? In other words, will the users be able to benefit from the system, and will they find it easy to do so? Any choice that would compromise this criterion will ultimately jeopardize the likely success of the project.

Hardware Considerations

Expert systems can be delivered on a wide variety of platforms, including personal computers (PCs), minicomputers, and mainframes. The choice depends on the availability of existing hardware in the organization or jurisdiction and the projected use of the system. Consideration has to be given to several areas:

1. Will the system require multi-user access? If this is not a requirement, hardware selection can be based on other factors. Multi-user access is

advantageous if the users (e.g., detectives) are decentralized, or if there are multiple users such as dispatchers. The multi-user problem is different if it is a question of remote access versus simultaneous access. The former is easily handled; the latter is not.

2. Is the existing computer system overloaded, and can access be given to the users on a need-to-use basis? Expert systems are primarily operational in nature and hence do not necessarily follow fixed reporting schedules. That may cause a conflict with the priorities and usage procedures of existing systems.

3. Does the expert system have to be linked to the police information system? In the long run, all of the data held by a department are shared, and, thus, isolating the expert system database outside the standard case management system is inefficient. In the short run, however, the tools and mind-set necessary for developing intelligent systems are in short supply in mainframe environments. It is clear that the embedded model is the correct one if it can be accomplished. This is especially true for dispatch systems that serve multiple departments.

Software Considerations

The software can be written in conventional languages like FORTRAN, C, COBOL, and Pascal. It also may be written in the languages of artificial intelligence--LISP or PROLOG. The selection of the software package is also influenced by a number of factors.

First, there is the possibility of using an expert system shell, a number of which offer a collection of capabilities; they can input a series of production rules and facts, collect data from the user, run the inference engine, and produce a set of conclusions. They vary in price, efficiency, and level of sophistication. Potential limitations include the number of rules allowed, the ability to take data from external databases and spreadsheets, the forms of knowledge representation provided (e.g. rules, frames), the type of control strategies used by the inference engine, and the quality of the user interface and graphics available in a finished product.

The shells found on workstations and large PCs are generally more sophisticated than those found in mainframe environments, although this is changing. Thus, it is useful to consider one of the PC-based shells as a vehicle for the initial prototyping and implementation even if the ultimate target is a large systems environment. This is also a useful strategy in cases where the ultimate system will be distributed in environments represented by the average PC (as opposed to the workstation PC).

Second, there is the question of integrating the power of expert systems shells with other conventional software so as to take advantage of the efficiencies of each. This is an area for imagination and creativity. Three different solutions were used in the burglary, dispatch, and career criminal expert systems.

In the burglary project, which worked with a large database of incidents and arrests, there was a need for local data entry and quality control on the input. Shells are less efficient at performing "data processing" tasks. Therefore, the development and processing of the knowledge base was handled by Gold Works, a shell provided by Gold Hill Computers. That side of the development was done in LISP. The conventional side of the system, which stores and processes the burglary data, was written in C and takes advantage of a conventional database management system. The system passes the data to the expert system, which makes its inferences, and then passes those inferences back to the conventional data-processing system as additional data elements. This model is that of an embedded expert system. Although the implementation was done on large-scale personal computers (80386 class processor), the same model could hold equally well for mainframe systems.

The career criminal system is, in large part, text driven since the output is a plan for a career criminal-repeat offender program. It was developed totally in the Gold Works shell, although the ultimate environment is the standard personal computer. This prototyping strategy allows for significant modification of the knowledge base in the early stages, a task that would be much more difficult in a conventional programming language. The knowledge base and inference engine-oriented debugging tools found in the shells are enormously helpful in finding flaws in the rules and procedures. Once the system is stable, it can be rewritten in C to reduce the required memory from 8 megabytes to 640K. A number of products are available to help in this task. These products take rules as input and generate the required C source statements and inference engine. The generated code can then be integrated with the balance of the conventionally developed system.

The prototype dispatcher expert system was developed totally in C without the assistance of any of the shells or C generators. That decision was made in part because of the demands of the other components of the system and in part because it is a true multi-user system, and that is a problem not addressed by the workstations and PC shells. In retrospect, the system would have benefited if the subsystem had first been prototyped in an AI shell.

Of primary importance is the technical competence of the systems users. If they are operational personnel, such as detectives, or dispatchers, then the software should provide as user friendly an environment as possible. This means that the software selection must take into consideration the users' level of expertise, even with PCs.

System Integration Considerations

Hardware and software considerations alone are not sufficient to develop a successful system. Integrating the technical aspects with the management and operations of the agencies is just as crucial for expert systems as it is for traditional information systems. The differences lie more in focus and emphasis than procedures.

If the system is supported by a data-processing unit, many of the technical problems associated with development and implementation are reduced. If, however, the system is to operate as a stand-alone, operated by the users, then not only is the software package important but so is the question of how it will be maintained. Clearly someone must be responsible for the care of the system. In the BCPD this responsibility has been given to a detective with computer interest and expertise. Additional technical support will have to be sought from outside consultants.

Training is an important factor in the implementation package since these systems are most often operationally oriented. One cannot expect the users to be "computer literate" in the beginning. Thus, time and opportunity will have to provided by the department to bring this about.

Finally, the operations of the system and its output have to be integrated with the other procedures in existence. For burglary detectives, the output should be used in conjunction with other leads that assist in crime-solving. For the dispatchers, some responses will still require approval. For the program planners and designers, the final program plan has to be acceptable to the heads of the agencies.

The involvement of users has to be consistent throughout each stage of the development and implementation process, for several reasons. The most compelling reason is that users are best suited to judge whether the results of the inferencing appear to be sensible. If the inferences are not "reasonable", the system will not be used. Only through involvement can the user explain why specific inferences were made. This is of crucial importance in the assessment of the validity of the rules since errant rules can be identified and peculiar results caused by the interaction of many rules can be isolated. In addition, users have good ideas. Designing a system with user input and keeping them involved throughout the process enhances the rule-making and inferencing processes. One clear example is in the residential burglary system, which can ignore certain rules if the user does not agree with the conclusion reached. With respect to a given case, some users wanted the capability of temporarily modifying or deleting some data elements if they had a low level of confidence in the reported data and also wanted the ability to construct dummy cases with only the key data they felt were relevant. All of these capabilities alter the output of the expert system, and the user has the final responsibility for selecting the appropriate course of action.

The implementation of an expert system can take many forms and can be based on the best hardware and software selections, but without the involvement of users during all the steps, the system has decidedly lower probabilities for success.

VALIDATION AND MODIFICATION

Even after the implementation process is complete and the initial validation has been completed, there will be a need for continuous monitoring of the system and subsequent alteration of the knowledge base. This must be expected and planned for, especially even if the users will be able to maintain the system themselves.

In the best of all worlds, the system should monitor itself. As data are added to the database and inferences are run, the system should be able to check its inferences against actual data. Certainty factors can be updated in this fashion, and rules that do not pass the certainty threshold for utilization (usually 70%) will no longer be permitted to fire.

In the burglary system, this means checking the generated profile against the observed profile when the individual is arrested. For the dispatch system, the action taken should be compared against the action suggested. In both cases, the certainty factors associated with the rules can be dynamically updated to reflect these comparisons. Rules that do not pass a certain threshold of truth will be turned off.

The more difficult task is adding new rules to the knowledge base after the original engineering has been completed. This may be physically possible if the system uses an expert system shell and the data necessary to fire the rule is already present in the database. Even if the data are in the system and the user knows physically how to add a rule, caution is needed if the user does not understand the structure that the knowledge engineer built. In the case where the data are not in the database needed to fire the rule, more drastic changes may be required. For systems written in conventional languages where the knowledge base is hard-coded, the problem of updating is even more severe.

The modification of the knowledge base is likely to be a more difficult problem for the dispatch system than for the burglary system. While there may be a desire to expand the burglary profile elements to include deeper knowledge, it is likely that all of the data elements would be in the database. In the case of dispatch, the situation is likely to be more volatile. Both resource types (e.g., acquisition of a helicopter) and rules for utilizing resources are quite likely to change. Due consideration should be given to this factor when designing the knowledge base.

Perhaps the more interesting possibility is the potential for the system to suggest new rules based on the analysis of the raw data through induction. Whether this will prove to be practical is unknown, but the potential is real, and when it becomes possible, the validation and update mechanisms will play a more important role in keeping the system viable. For now, it is probably enough to solve the problems of creating a working expert system.

CONCLUSION

There are a number of places in which an expert system can get into trouble. Of these, the most crucial are:

1. Picking a very difficult or a trivial problem.
2. Underestimating time and resources needed to produce a usable system.

3. Choosing a disinterested expert or one incapable of expressing their procedures.
4. Providing an inadequate user interface or inferences that are not credible.

Any of these problems--and many others--can sink a project. Probably the best approach is to start small and bootstrap your way into this technology. It may be difficult to get a second chance.

5

SOME FUNDAMENTALS OF ARTIFICIAL INTELLIGENCE

AI as a field is barely thirty years old, with its roots beginning in the 1950's. Both an art and a science, it is concerned with the study of systems that exhibit some characteristic of intelligent behavior, such as language, problem solving, or learning. The field has evolved from its early fascination with game playing and theorem proving to emphasizing practical applications perhaps best represented by the techniques employed in many expert systems.

AI research is concerned with more than applications. For years researchers largely ignored applications, preferring to concentrate on the more theoretical aspects of the field. In the 1980's it became increasingly evident that if the field was to be taken seriously, it would have to move some concepts out of the lab and into practice.

Expert systems represented by MYCIN and XCON, among others, proved to be the best path for AI researchers to show the utilitarian side of their work. The applications discussed in this book are an extension of that process. To suggest that this process has been smooth and trouble free would be inaccurate. In fact, all the hype and unfulfilled promises of these systems have caused both public institutions and private companies to draw back from their headlong plunge into these applications. It is clear that there are powerful methods represented in expert systems and that those methods will take their rightful place with structured programming, relational databases, and other paradigms.

This chapter provides a summary of AI research to show the place that expert systems occupy within the broad spectrum of AI.

OVERVIEW

AI is generally concerned with studying the way humans use their brains, and in particular how computers are used as a medium for simulating and understanding that phenomenon. It is easy to get embroiled in an argument as to whether machines programmed to exhibit or simulate behavior normally ascribed to human beings are intelligent. For our purposes, it does not matter. If the computer produces results similar to those expected from humans, it is probably useful, and that is probably where the argument should end.

The AI field is broad. It ranges from problem solving, which is, in part, represented by expert systems, through natural languages, robotics, automatic programming, and machine learning. Some of the fields have been more successful than others at producing applications, that is simulating human behavior. To a large extent, all of the subfields support one another and borrow tools and concepts from each other. They all share common technologies and AI methods.

Natural Languages

Natural language research is concerned with a range of topics, including machine translation of text from one language to another (such as French to English), grammar, and parsing. The utility of machine translation is obvious, but it has had an uneven developmental history, causing research in the area to be abandoned from time to time as the work became too difficult. Recently, however, it has made a big comeback, with some commercial companies, machines, and software specializing in this function.

To understand the content of a sentence, one must understand something about grammar. A machine trying to understand and act on input in the form of a language must be able to do the same. Research in grammar focuses on how to understand the structure of the language presented to a machine usually as a series of text strings. There are several different approaches to grammar, but fundamentally all must accomplish the task of matching the input against a knowledge base of rules governing the language. One of the applications of this research is a grammar checker, which has recently joined spellers in the word-processing market.

The parser has the job of decoding the input language. In simple systems, this may amount to comparing each word to its dictionary and determining if it knows the word. If it knows the word, it may then identify it as a noun, verb, adjective, or other part of speech. The sequence of words may then be used to build a structure or tree, which fully represents the input. If the parser is successful in constructing the tree, the problem is reduced to determining whether some response should be generated by this input. One application of this research is answering questions posed in ordinary English. The parser interprets the question and extracts the appropriate data from a database. Another application might scan text and build abstracts from source documents.

This field is important for a variety of reasons, but its most significant application can be found in the improvement of man-machine dialogue. Most users of computers today must either learn the syntax that the application or operating system software understands or select items from a menu. Either can be restrictive, especially in the case where one needs to query a database. It is much more natural to ask, "What cities have a population over 1 million?" than to say "Select city-name from cities where population greater than 1,000,000." Ultimately this field of research will produce the truly user-friendly computer.

Computer Vision

Sight is certainly one of the most important inputs to human mental processes. We gather enormous amounts of information visually, and that input is central to human behavior. If machines are to be able to simulate even a small part of that behavior, vision is one sense that is vital.

The processing of visual information can be divided roughly into three parts: capturing the image, evaluating the picture that has been received, and if necessary, taking some action. For example, a person is observed crossing the street (an image is captured). That image is instinctively compared to others that are stored mentally (pattern recognition). If the person is recognized, we wave (understanding).

The usual device for gathering an image is either a single or multiple television cameras depending on whether two-dimensional or three-dimensional processing is required. The image is converted into a series of pixels, or dots, which in their simplest form (black or white) are on or off. This image may be subjected to further processing to clear out any extraneous information or noise, smoothing, adjustment for the angle of observation and lighting, and ultimately the determination of the overall outline of the image. The techniques used are akin to computer-enhanced imaging done in the space program and medical diagnosis.

The main work for AI lies in pattern recognition. Once the image has been cleaned up, it must be compared against the known patterns in the knowledge base. This may range from a simple template-matching process, which is probably the current limit for real-world applications, to attempts to account for overlapping objects and other similarly complex problems.

The applications of computer vision, especially as applied to robotics, attempt to simplify the process by carefully controlling how images are received. In this way, the scenes that have to be learned are relatively simple and avoid as much of the complexity as possible.

Robotics

Robotics is also a fertile area for the application of AI techniques. While we generally think of AI as simulating mental behavior, it is only a short step to convert the output of an intelligent system from a visual response on a screen to the controlled movement of an arm and/or hand. Robotics research and applications are concerned with the control and manipulation of physical devices to perform a variety of tasks. The simplest robots "know" one job and repeatedly execute that single task. We are familiar with automated manufacturing plants where many tasks such as welding and painting have passed from human to mechanical hands. Robotics are particularly important in doing jobs that are hazardous to human health.

More complex robots, which are intended to simulate more difficult human tasks, will require a series of sensors much as humans have. A human simultaneously gathers information by using all of the senses: sight, hearing, touch, smell, and taste. The key word is simultaneous. Most computers, however, act serially and not in parallel. Thus, the development of high-speed computers using many parallel processors is the key to the mythical android of science-fiction. Some robots can "see" using television cameras. Visual information is gathered for the purpose of pattern recognition. For example, a robot may have been taught that a properly machined part has a particular pattern or shape. The robot can look at the logic of the pattern and determine if it is correct. Alternatively, a robot may execute a different series of tasks depending on the visual image that has been captured.

Machine Learning

One of the most difficult problems for expert systems is keeping them up to date. Real experts learn new information as they encounter new situations or observe alternative outcomes. An expert system that does not change is missing one of the most fundamental characteristics of human behavior: the ability to learn and to change.

Machines can "learn" certain types of information easily. The multiplication tables and the capitals of the fifty states, for example, are easily programmed or codified in a database for future use. A program or a procedure can also easily be learned since it acts the same way each time. Humans have a collection of facts and procedures that they use routinely almost without thinking.

The more important type of learning is cognitive. We are continually observing and drawing conclusions based on limited information. We all know what a dog is, and we can recognize and classify an animal as a dog even though we may never before have observed the particular breed. This process of learning by example or induction is extremely important to humans. In fact, it probably accounts for a large number of the differences among people. If one individual makes a set of observations drawn from an environment that is totally different from that of a second person, there is no mystery as to why their generalizations may differ significantly.

The focus of AI research in this area is to make machines capable of observing a set of conditions and outcomes and modify or add to the knowledge base of the application based upon those observations. This work is of particular interest in the knowledge acquisition stage of building expert systems, always a real bottleneck.

Problem Solving

Generally, we are involved in two types of problem solving. First, we solve some problems mathematically or computationally, such as balancing the checkbook or determining the time until lunch. But a wide range of problems cannot be solved computationally: What is the best route to take on vacation? Where is the best place to buy a new car? What type of investments should I consider? For these problems we use the second type of problem solving: we search for a solution. The search process may be complicated or simple. In some cases, any solution will suffice, in others, only the optimal solution will satisfy the search. Yes, you can find that identical new car at a number of dealerships, but will it be the best price with the best delivery date? The ways humans solve such problems is of critical importance in AI research.

Expert systems represent one application of the problem-solving methods of AI research. Such systems search for a solution using a large amount of domain knowledge stored in a largely unstructured manner, at least when compared to the more familiar tree structures. Although large advances have been made in knowledge representation and knowledge acquisition, consultative systems have many difficulties to resolve. Still, such systems will continue to be constructed because they satisfy part of the larger, continuing need for consultants and ultimately trainers.

TOOLS OF ARTIFICIAL INTELLIGENCE

The expert system uses two AI methodologies that differentiate it from the typical data-processing or computational system: *search*--the process by which the system reaches a solution to a problem, and *knowledge representation*--the manner in which the domain knowledge gathered from experts is stored to support the search for a solution. These two concepts are integrated within the typical expert system.

Search

Although the dimensions of search are derived from the game-playing research done in the early years, the activity is serious; it is at the core of expert systems research. Search has three basic components: (1) a searchspace over which the search is conducted, (2) a set of actions or operators that can be taken, and (3) alternative reasoning and search method(s). The object is to find the solution to a problem found within a search space by using a set of "operators" through a reasoning method utilizing a search strategy.

This may seem a bit abstract, so consider the following example. You are at the entry to a maze, and your goal is to exit the maze at the other side. At each decision point, you may take one of several actions (or use one of several operators): go forward, go back, go left, or go right. After your initial decision, you ask, "Am I done?" If you are not, then you apply another one of the operators and continue to search. This procedure is known as *generate and test*. The search space is the maze. The reasoning process described is forward or data-driven reasoning. No particular search strategy is demonstrated.

The search space is the area over which the search is to be conducted. Conceptually this is an important point, since a poorly defined search space may not contain the solution to the problem. In a chess game or a game of checkers, the search space is well defined. In the case of a sexual assault in a private residence, the search space might be limited by the set of all known sex offenders, but in reality the offender was a burglar and the assault was incidental to the burglary. If the search is to be successful, the expert will quickly narrow the search space within which the solution is most likely to be found.

There are three ways of representing search spaces: as a state space, by problem reduction, or as a game tree. State space representation is based on the principle that each action taken leads to exactly one new state, which is generally less complicated than the previous state. If you think of the state space as a graph or tree that has at its top many choices or branches to take, then as you move along the graph, the options are fewer because previous paths have been bypassed.

The problem-reduction representation has as its primary characteristic the division of the main problem into many subproblems. Each subproblem must be solved before the main problem can be solved. In fact, each subproblem may cause decomposition into other subproblems that must also be solved before its parent can be solved.

Game trees must be represented in a different way since there is more than one player. They are analogous to the typical chess game. Each player must consider not only the current state of the board, the actions that his or her pieces can take, and the ultimate solution, checkmate, but also the set of actions the opposing player can take. In other words, after the piece is moved, the player may be confronted by any number of different states represented by the countermove.

Every problem-solving situation has a set of operators or actions with which to move through the search space. In a game of checkers, forward, backward, and diagonal moves are permitted. In a chess game, each piece has a set of moves associated with it. In every case the operators are the method by which the search for a goal or solution is carried out.

There are three general reasoning methods by which we reach any given conclusion: forward, backward, and bidirectional reasoning. Forward reasoning is data driven. That is, it looks at the available data, makes decisions about how to proceed, and continues this process until ultimately the solution to the problem is found. For example, a detective examines all the elements of a burglary to gain insight about the offender. Some of the elements are rejected as not important; other leads are followed up. The solution is to identify the burglar. This is forward reasoning. (See Figure 5.1)

Backward reasoning follows the opposite logic. It knows the desired solution and then examines the data to determine whether they are consistent with the outcome. Problem-reduction representation usually uses backward reasoning since it is goal driven as opposed to data driven. A CAD system may use this type of reasoning when it knows that an immediate response to a call for service is warranted, and it checks each possible solution within the search space (available car) to determine if it fits the parameters to respond. The solution is satisfied if the available data fit the selected conclusion. That is the backward-reasoning process. (See Figure 5.2)

Bidirectional search uses both methods to reach the solution. It simultaneously starts one search at the top and another at the goal. When the two searches intersect, the solution has been found. Parts of the career criminal expert system can be developed with this type of reasoning as modifications are made to procedures and policies supporting the goals of the program.

In addition to the type of reasoning used in a search, there are also different search strategies that can be employed. The maze example best exemplifies the blind search method. Since we have no information about which path is the most promising, we can choose one of two strategies for getting through the maze: depth-first or breadth-first. (See Figure 5.3)

The depth-first approach will continue down a single path until it arrives at the goal or the path is identified as a blind alley. At that point, a second path is chosen, and it too is followed to its ultimate conclusion. This strategy follows until the goal (exit of the maze) is found. The difficulty with this approach is that it can produce an early solution, but it may not necessarily be the shortest route. There is also the theoretical possibility that one can follow a single path forever and never reach a solution. (See Figure 5.4)

The breadth-first strategy does not follow each path to its greatest depth. Instead it follows each and every path to its next decision point. Suppose the maze begins with three possible paths to follow. Each of those paths then splits again, and so forth. The breadth-first strategy would follow each of the three paths to the next level. This strategy would ensure

Figure 5.1

Reasoning Methods
Forward Reasoning

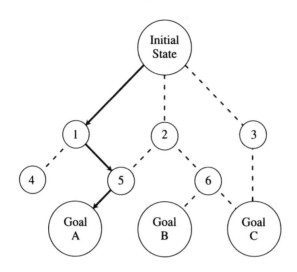

Figure 5.2

Reasoning Methods
Backward Reasoning

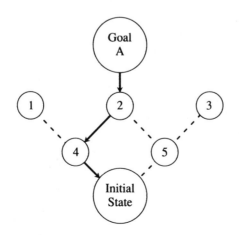

Figure 5.3

Search Strategies
Breadth First

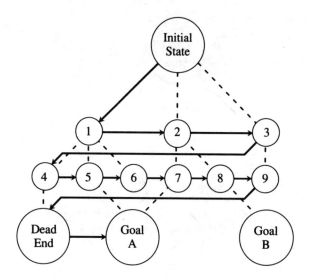

Figure 5.4

Search Strategies
Depth First

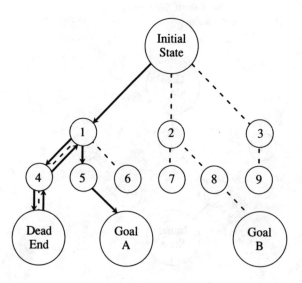

finding the shortest route, at least in terms of decisions or actions, but it might take a long time to do so.   The   expert detective at a burglary scene will usually begin with a breadth first strategy to ensure that there is not some obvious short, quick solution. Then he or she will choose the most promising line of inquiry and follow that until it leads to a solution or is abandoned. In some cases the investigator may do a mental run through of a series of known suspects and determine if the observed data fit any of those goals.

There are other variations, which place additional costs on individual paths and provide other reasons for choosing among paths.   Still, all of these strategies suffer from the possibility of combinatorial explosion.   Without information about how to search, there could be an endless set of paths for one to search before reaching a conclusion.

The analogy to burglary detectives is obvious. While one detective may follow a lead to its logical conclusion (the depth-first strategy), another may be examining all clues and evidence to determine which leads would be best to follow (breadth-first strategy). In both instances, there is always the possibility that the offender may never be identified or arrested.

The best-first search strategy uses an evaluation function to measure the likelihood that a particular decision or action will lead to the desired goal.   This function will generally estimate the distance between each node and the ultimate goal. One commonly used function is the A^* algorithm, which uses cost as well as distance to discriminate between decisions.

Heuristic search addresses the problem of combinatorial explosion and the inefficiencies of the two previous search strategies.   Heuristic search uses a best-first strategy wherein rules of thumb or evaluation functions help select the path to follow.   In the blind searches outlined above, there is no particular reason for choosing any one path of several presented. In heuristic searches, prior knowledge is used to choose a path. If there is a way of making an informed decision about which path is more likely to lead to a solution, the risk of that decision's being wrong would be worth accepting.

Heuristic search introduces the idea of domain expertise into the process. Humans routinely limit the search space when trying to reach a goal and make informed judgments about the path they should follow. They are, in general, willing to accept the risk of being wrong in order to reach the goal in a shorter time. They also routinely make midcourse corrections if they perceive a shorter or cheaper route. It is this human activity that is incorporated into the heuristic search strategies.

Continuing with the analogy, the experienced and knowledgeable burglary detective knows that matching fingerprints offers a more likely means for identifying a burglar than tracing any stolen property. Sometimes the entire search strategy can be short-circuited if the M.O. of the burglar is unique and he is instantly identified by his "signature."

It would appear from this discussion that all the various paths from the initial state to the final goal for any problem can be mapped. Yet this is not necessarily the case, nor do experts usually think in this manner. As a result, there has been increasing interest in how the experts do think and how knowledge can be represented.

Knowledge Representation

Knowledge representation is the second key methodology. In any expert system project, one or more methods of knowledge representation will be used. Two methods--rules and frames--were mentioned briefly in chapter 4. But there are a number of others, including propositional and predicate logic, semantic nets, and hierarchies. In this section, we will discuss each of these alternatives and some of their characteristics. Any might be considered by the knowledge engineer when selecting software for building the expert system.

Production Rules

Rules, the core of a production system, are extensively used in expert systems. They are a natural way for people to express information. The if-then construct allows the construction of either simple or complex relationships depending on the number of antecedent conditions. This works fine for procedural or action-type knowledge but is inefficient or even inadequate for nonprocedural or less action-oriented types of knowledge. In that case, additional forms of representation may be employed.

Rule-based systems are convenient and easy to understand in practice, but too often they are implemented in a completely unstructured fashion. The statement is often made that it is easy to add or delete rules from such systems, and that is true. But this can lead to unrecognized conflicts and the need for resolution strategies. One can arrange rules to fire in a precise order to simulate a network or tree structure by assigning priorities. This may or may not be desirable. In practice, it is better to avoid a completely unstructured set of rules. The judicious use of priorities, meta-rules, and rule sets that are activated only under certain circumstances will undoubtedly improve this form of representation.

Frames

Frames are similar to the description of a record in a database except that the capabilities associated with a frame are far more extensive. Instead of having a person record in a database, there is a person frame in a knowledge base. The frame is composed of slots that are comparable to fields. A slot in the person frame might be the sex of the person. A slot can also contain more complex information such as: a default value, or a procedure to be called if the field is required but is missing; if the data is changed; or, if it is constrained such as ONE-OF (male,female). A slot may also contain more than one symbol; for example, the occupation slot may contain the symbols (POLICE_OFFICER, SOLDIER, INTERPRETER . . .).

Frames provide a convenient way of ordering knowledge through inheritance. A second frame, called "criminal," might contain slots such as criminal identification number, current status, and date last arrested. A "child of the person" frame will inherit all of the slots in the person frame as well. In cases where multiple inheritance is permitted, a frame may be a child of more than one parent frame. This frame structure is quite convenient for holding data in a production system. In the burglary system, frames were created for the crime and criminal and a variety of child frames.

Frames are only definitions of structures; they do not explicitly hold the data. The data for an actual person would be an "instance" of the person frame. Thus, each new burglary becomes part of working memory through a process called *instantiation*, or the attaching of specific values to an object. These values may be referenced as part of either the antecedent or the consequent of a production rule.

Logic

Another way of representing knowledge in an expert system is logic. Propositional logic is a method of analyzing the truth, or lack thereof, of new propositions. New propositions are formed from known propositions using Boolean operators such as AND, OR, NOT, IMPLIES, and EQUIVALENCE. We are all familiar with these operators and their effect. Given two propositions--for example, the burglar is young, the burglar takes

Figure 5.5

**Comparison of True/False Combinations
with IMPLY Operator**

	True/False Combinations		IMPLY Operator	
	Window	Young	Window	Young
1.	F	F	F	T
2.	F	T	F	T
3.	T	F	T	F
4.	T	T	T	T

only cash--the OR operator says that the combined proposition "burglar is young OR burglar takes only cash" is true if *either* of its components is true. In the same way, "burglar is young AND burglar takes only cash" produces a true result only if *both* propositions are true. The IMPLIES operator has a more complex result. The statement "burglar takes only cash IMPLIES burglar is young" will be true if the burglar is young *or* the burglar does not take cash.

To illustrate, suppose we assert that "burglar enters through a window IMPLIES burglar was young." We can question whether one can be deduced from the other because it is logically consistent. This is done by expressing every possible combination in a truth table and examining under what circumstances one implies the other. Figure 5.5 shows how the IMPLIES operator allows one to deduce truth under these conditions.

Row 1 is true because the IMPLIES operator allows the inverse of consistent statements to be true: the entry was not made by window, so the criminal is not young. Row 2 is also true; the entry was not made by the window, but the burglar is young, and is allowed under the IMPLIES operator. Row 3 says that entry was made by window, and the burglar was not young, which is false. In the fourth row, entry was made by window, and he was young, which is true.

Thus, the use of discrete statements and the appropriate operators provides a method for making inferences about the truthfulness of new propositions. It should be clear, however, that constructing truth tables for complex propositions can produce quite large and cumbersome tables. Further, the propositions can only be tested for truth according to rules of logic, not whether they are true in practice.

Predicate logic attempts to overcome many of the shortcomings of propositional logic and at the same time retain the fundamental mathematical rules. The typical statement includes a predicate and one or more arguments that are object. For example the statement that "Jones steals" could be represented by "Steals(Jones)," where *Steals* is the predicate and *Jones* is the object. The fact that Jones is a burglar would be represented as an assertion or fact: "burglar(Jones)." More complicated constructs like rules and frames can also be developed using predicate logic, the form of knowledge representation used in PROLOG.

Other Methods to Represent Knowledge

Semantic networks are used to represent knowledge graphically. The graphs consist of nodes that represent objects of interest (things, people, actions, concepts) and connecting links. These networks are particularly useful for showing inheritance. Given the information that Herman is a fence, there might be nodes for person, drug seller, stolen property, fence. Connecting links would show that Herman is a person; Herman sells drugs; drugs are paid for with stolen property; and stolen property is sold to the syndicate. Thus, anything known about drugs and stolen property can be inferred or inherited by Herman.

The nodes and relationships can be represented symbolically in the computer, and then the ability to answer questions is once again a problem of search. Questions such as "Does Herman receive stolen property?" can be answered by following the paths through the things that Herman does until we deduce that the answer is yes because Herman is a fence and a fence receives stolen property for resale.

Scripts represent knowledge by describing a sequence of events. The sequence is described much as a play with actors, scenes, and props. The typical burglary might be described as four scenes: actions in target selection, entry, activity in the house, and exit. Several different variations of the script might be used depending on whether the house was occupied since different actions might be taken. Further, different variations might be used depending on the motive of the actor; for example, a need for money for drugs would require a different script than that for a professional antiques thief. With the initial conditions satisfied, a script is selected, and questions can be addressed to the script. The script requires little or no input data other than that the situation for validating the script exists.

USING PRODUCTION RULES

The popularity of production rules as a form of knowledge representation stems from two sources. First, it is somewhat easier to get experts to organize and express their thoughts in the if-then production rule form. This certainly simplifies the knowledge acquisition process in comparison to some other procedures that require a more complete specification of the problem-solving process, such as a diagram or network. The second reason for this choice is that programmers find it relatively easy to build systems expressed using this format in conventional languages or to build shells that process knowledge expressed as a rule. The mechanism for coordinating these activities in an expert system application is the *inference engine*. The inference engine processes rules uses one of three methods of chaining; searches the knowledge base; and controls the order of the rule firing.

In processing rules, the inference engine works on a recognize-and-act cycle. At any point in time, working memory contains all of the knowledge about the system. This knowledge is usually represented as a list of some sort. For example, one piece of information might represent the fact that in INCIDENT1, the break-in was through the window. In working memory, this might be represented as (INCIDENT1 ENTRY WINDOW). There might also be a rule that says, "If the entry was through the window, then the criminal was young." The inference engine will usually check each active rule (some rules may not be active at any given point in time) in the system. If its antecedent (the *if* part) matches information in working memory, then either the consequent (the *then* part) is asserted (added to working memory), or the rule is put on an agenda to be processed later.

Parallel to the reasoning methods discussed earlier, inference engines use one of three methods of chaining: forward, backward, or mixed. The most common is forward chaining. The example used is that of forward chaining; that is, the rule is processed from the data side (antecedent) rather than the goal side (consequent).

Backward chaining also has a role to play. In backward chaining, the inference engine examines the knowledge base for rules that match a goal that it has been given and then determines if the antecedent conditions have been met. If the goal exists but the antecedent is not known, it looks for rules where the antecedent in the first rule is the consequent of a second rule. For example, suppose rule 1 says, "If entry was through the window, then the age of the criminal was young," and rule 2 states, "If the door was not used, then entry was through a window." If the system is asked, "Was the criminal young?" then the backward chain would start with the consequent of rule 1 and attempt to determine if that was a known fact or the antecedent of rule 1 is true. If either case is true, the conclusion is immediately reached. Otherwise the inference engine finds that if rule 2 were true, then rule 1 would be true. The search is then continued to prove rule 2. If rule 2 is true, the inference engine will assert that entry was through the window and then can assert that the criminal was young.

A mixed strategy might be followed in complex situations whereby a backward-chaining strategy is coupled with the enabling of forward rules to infer data where none exists to complete the chain.

The description of forward and backward chaining looks much like backward (inductive) and forward (deductive) reasoning; however, it is not. Chaining is a method of firing rules, and either approach can be used to implement either type of reasoning.

The selection of a particular method of chaining is dependent on the application and the tools available in the shell, if one is being used. Backward chaining is used primarily in diagnostic systems where a symptom has been observed and one is trying to ascertain the data consistent with that condition. It is also appropriate when the number of goals are relatively fewer than the initial states (an upside-down pyramid). Forward chaining is utilized in situations where data are sparse and knowledge is rich (pyramid). In that case, the problem is to infer as much information (as possible as opposed to limiting the search space, as happens in backward chaining).

The inference engine searches the knowledge base using various methods. It can do a depth-first search, which means it will follow a single chain until it succeeds or fails, and then pursue the second line of inquiry. Alternatively, it can follow both paths, a single level at a time, until one or both are accepted or rejected. In backward chaining, for example, there may be more than one consequent that matches the goal (the defendant was young).

The inference engine is also concerned with control of the process. After it has identified all the rules that could be fired, it directs its attention to the question of the order in which they should fire. The results of the inference process may change significantly if the order of rule firing is altered because working memory is continually being altered.

Different inference engines have different methods of making the choice. They will generally fall into one of four categories. The first approach essentially marks a rule as having fired so that it may not fire again unless a new set of data is introduced. The second strategy is to select the rule that has the freshest or most recent data as part of its antecedent. This is possible since most systems keep a tag associated with each item in working memory telling when it entered. The third method is to select the rule that has the specific or restrictive antecedent. For example, if rule 1 has a single condition in its antecedent and rule 2 has more conditions that must be met, then fire rule 2. Finally, many systems will allow the developer to assign priorities for rule firing so that the higher-priority item will fire first.

The control strategies used in the inference engine are provided as a way of simplifying the implementation of the expert system. Still, the developer may introduce rules in the system that provide additional control. This employs the concept of meta-knowledge, or knowledge about knowledge. For example, the design may suggest that a certain set of rules apply only in specific situations. If the crime is burglary, then rules 1-100 are valid; otherwise, use 101-150. This strategy can be used to make sure that inferencing about a subproblem is completed before rules about the overall problem are activated. Essentially the expert is clarifying how and under what circumstances the knowledge should be used.

Despite the ease with which production rule systems can be constructed, there are a number of potential problems that should be emphasized. One of the main advantages of the production rule system relative to other forms of knowledge representation is that it is easy to add new information to the knowledge base because each rule is discrete and is entered in an unstructured environment. But there is a difficulty: there is no mechanism to prevent the entry of arbitrary rules that are in direct conflict with others. There is also no guarantee that the on-board conflict-resolution mechanism in the inference engine will produce the right firing order to reproduce the expert's opinion. This problem also points out the need to work with the expert in determining the proper control strategy and sequencing where some nonarbitrary reasoning process is at work.

6
DATA PROCESSING AND THE EXPERT SYSTEM

The development of an expert system or the desire to develop one by a line organization can cause friction with more traditional data-processing (DP) support organizations. The reactions cover the spectrum from outright opposition and disruption, through ambivalence and disinterest, to positive, enthusiastic support.

The reasons for this variety of attitudes are understandable. First, the user is developing a technology that is more advanced in many ways than that provided by DP professionals. Second, the languages and the jargon of AI are rarely encountered by mainstream programmers and systems analysts. Third, new and probably expensive equipment is being added to the users' department without the advice and consent of the DP department. In many cases, the new hardware will be viewed as superior to that normally provided by DP. Fourth, after the consultants and researchers have gone, DP ultimately may have to provide support for a system in which they had little input. Finally, although DP is generally regarded as the keeper of the organizational database and systems, expert systems are more likely to be located in user departments, outside the control of DP. These circumstances may create severe misgivings in the typical DP director.

These issues are clearly observable in law enforcement agencies where the police have a strong need for highly integrated information systems. They use their databases extensively and require information quickly, often in real time. Thus, a major issue in the long run is how to integrate expert systems with the mainframe-based databases. The degree of integration may dictate fully embedded expert systems; it may also allow for stand-alone workstations serviced by a mainframe file server or periodic downloads. At stake is the degree to which the system is kept up-to-date. Until a true distributed database is available, centralized input and update of shared data are mandatory. While separate systems can exist in the short run as the prototype expert system is developed, security and data sharing demand a centralized repository for most police data in the long run.

Whatever solution is adopted, either in the short or long run, DP will ultimately take on a new role as it integrates this tool with others under its care. Depending on the model developed, the AI languages used, and the manner in which existing databases are integrated with the ones used by the expert system, DP will have to become aware of and familiar with this new weapon in the war against crime.

To provide a background to this changing systems environment, this chapter presents a discussion of two areas important to DP managers: languages in AI and organizational databases. This discussion should help reduce some of the more prevalent concerns that DP may have and shed some light on the relationships that are needed in the long run to develop working expert systems in a DP environment.

LANGUAGES OF ARTIFICIAL INTELLIGENCE

An expert system can be developed in one (or more) of several languages. Although the expert system shells advertise that one does not have to know a language to use the shell, that rarely will prove to be true. Elementary systems may use a standard menu interface to ease the development task, but it is rarely good for more than a prototype. The production version of the system will have to be written at least in part in a programming language.

In this section we explore some of the alternatives available and discuss their relative strengths and weaknesses. In this manner, some of the major issues can be clarified and some of the questions that MIS programmers might have about this field can be addressed.

LISP

LISP, the list processing language, has been the programming language of choice, at least in the United States, for applications using AI since the field began. It is a declarative language, a characteristic it shares with PROLOG.

That differentiates it from a procedural language like C, FORTRAN, and COBOL. LISP and PROLOG are concerned with what a task is, not how the task is to solved. In a procedural language, extracting a list of persons arrested within the last thirty days will require a procedure: for example (1) read an arrest record; (2) determine if the record is less than thirty days old; (3) if it is, print it out; (4) if not, at the end of the file, repeat the four steps. A nonprocedural language will simply supply a query, such as "select all from arrest where elapsed-time < 30 days." From this one should not conclude that LISP is devoid of procedural capabilities. In fact, it has an array of tools with which to tackle tasks that are best handled procedurally.

The power of LISP as an AI research language lies in two areas: its ability to manipulate symbolic information; and the programming environment within which one develops LISP programs. That environment is interpretive and fully interactive. Dynamic memory allocation is perhaps its most powerful feature. That is, the developer does not have to define every symbol formally and allocate its storage location in memory before using that symbol. This simplifies the program development process.

In addition, LISP is unique among languages in that a program is also data. All LISP programs are also lists. As such they may be read in by other LISP programs. This is a particularly important feature in the AI world because it means that programs can change themselves. This feature has a direct bearing on the subfields of automatic programming and machine learning.

LISP uses S-expressions. These expressions include atoms (numbers or symbols), lists, or a combination of one or more atoms or lists. Thus, BURGLAR is an atom, (BURGLAR) is a list of one atom, (BURGLAR JOHN) is a list, and (ENTERS BURGLAR (WINDOW DOOR)) is a list. Even arithmetic is handled as a list: (+ 1 2) adds 2 to 1. 1 and 2 are both atoms. Even an empty list ( ) is useful.

LISP knows about a number of primitives or functions. These primitives are used to process lists or atoms. CAR or FIRST is used to access the first element in a list. So (CAR '(ENTERS BURGLAR (WINDOW DOOR))) produces the result ENTERS. CDR or REST is used to extract the remainder. (CDR '(ENTERS BURGLAR (WINDOW DOOR))) produces (BURGLAR (WINDOW DOOR)). The second item in a list might be extracted by (CAR(CDR'(ENTERS BURGLAR

(WINDOW DOOR)))) produces BURGLAR. By using these primitives, any item within a list can be accessed.

In its simplest form, the database might contain two entries: (ENTERS JOHN (WINDOW DOOR)) and (ENTERS HARRY (DOOR)). If the user wants to know who enters by the window, the database could be checked for the atom WINDOW in a list and then extract the second symbol to get the name. The database may also have entries such as (JOHN HARRY), (ENTERS (WINDOW DOOR) TAKES (CASH VALUABLES) TARGETS (SINGLE-FAMILY UNOCCUPIED)). The first list may be the contents of a symbol BURGLARS, and the second list may be the contents of JOHN. In other words, BURGLARS = (JOHN HARRY) and JOHN = (ENTERS (WINDOW DOOR) TAKES (CASH VALUABLES) TARGETS (SINGLE-FAMILY UNOCCUPIED)). This allows the processing of the BURGLARS list and the subsequent checking of the contents of each burglar symbol for the appropriate information.

Other primitives are available to combine two lists (APPEND); add an element to a list (CONS); and create new lists (LIST). The actual value of a symbol can be set by SETQ-- SETQ BURGLARS '(JOHN HARRY) assigns a list to the symbol. Primitives also handle basic arithmetic, test for the type of a symbol--for example, (NUMBERP X) would determine if the X contained a number--and check for various Boolean conditions (EQUAL, GREATERP, and LESSP). COND is the primary primitive for if-then situations.

Functions are built using DEFUN. Functions use primitives of the type already described and other functions already defined by the developer to build new functions. These functions may be recursive, that is call themselves. This feature is useful for handling iterative situations. Conventional iteration can be handled by the LOOP primitive.

There are other specialized functions, such as EVAL, APPLY, MAPCAR, LAMBDA, READ, and others all used for specific purposes. The typical LISP environment also has a large number of other functions that have been predefined for easing the software development process.

It should be apparent by now that whatever structures we build and procedures we use, they will work on lists. LISP has no built-in pattern-matching routine, inference engine, or searching mechanism, but they can be constructed with the tools available. There is no built-in frame system for representing knowledge, however, a frame can be constructed as a complex list. Tree structures can be built as a series of lists where each node contains the value of its successors.

Probably the chief advantage that a developer who is used to working in a conventional language will notice is the ease of the write, test, and debug processes. The ability to program without initial declarations or typing of data is quite useful, and the ability to examine the contents of any variable easily at any time is most helpful. However, garbage collection--the way LISP recovers memory for other uses--can be annoying.

Structurally, the typical LISP program looks like a list of disconnected functions. However, it is not at all unlike a program written in C with a very short main program. If we view LISP as a prototyping tool, then the structure, execution speed, garbage collection, and special environments are not problems.

PROLOG

PROLOG (programming in logic) was developed in Europe and is still the language of choice among European and Japanese AI researchers. Like LISP, it is a declarative language; unlike LISP, it has a built-in inference engine with backtracking, pattern matching, and a search algorithm. It also has a standard way of handling data, which means that we do not have to be concerned with developing frames or other methods of knowledge representation. This enables the developer to write a system more rapidly than in LISP, assuming that the application fits the available tools. Given all of these resident features, it would appear that the only missing elements for an expert system are the database and the knowledge base. With those elements present, we should be able to interrogate the database.

Facts are represented by predicates. A predicate establishes the relationship between the argument(s) that follow. For example, if we know that John steals property, this would be expressed by "steals(JOHN PROPERTY)." With that information in the database, a question might be asked "? steals(JOHN PROPERTY)," at which point PROLOG would respond with "yes." Suppose a second fact was added: "steals(HARRY PROPERTY)." If the query was rephrased to "? steals(X, PROPERTY)," the search would return X = JOHN and X = HARRY). A third fact states that "property_type(PROPERTY, CASH_ONLY)." The response to "steals(JOHN, X), (X, CASH_ONLY)" or "What does John steal that is cash_only?" is X=property. The unification or instantiation of "property" as X satisfies both parts of the complex query.

Rules are encoded in a manner similar to the example given above. Suppose a rule states, "If a person is a burglar and the burglar enters through the window, then the person is young." This would be expressed in PROLOG as:

person(X, young) :-
person(X, burglar),
enters(X, window).

If the database contains the following facts,

enters(John, window)
person(John, burglar)

then the query "? person(John, young)," PROLOG would conclude that "yes," or that "person(John, young)." This conclusion is inferred from the rule since it is not in the database. The interpreter reaches this conclusion by backward chaining. It attempts first to see if there is a known fact that satisfies the goal; there is not. The rule, however, if true, would allow the interpreter to conclude that the goal is satisfied. This is accomplished by searching the database for a match on the first part of the rule, "person(X, burglar)," and finding that John fits the bill. The interpreter instantiates John as X and then proceeds to use X=John in the second part of the rule "enters(X, window." A match is found, and the inference is drawn.

If "person(John, burglar)" had not been a known fact and a rule had been present that

person(X, burglar):-
enters(X, window),
steals(X, property).

and the additional fact that "steals(John, property)" was known, then the backward chaining would have continued. Upon failing to find "person(John, burglar)" directly, the second rule would have been found that had the proper goal and its two component parts were true. That inference would then allow the ultimate goal to be proved.

PROLOG clearly has some substantial advantages in developing expert systems if the tools given fit the situation. If an alternate form of knowledge representation is needed or there is a need for substantial procedural programming, PROLOG may not fill the bill. It is, however, possible to develop forward chaining within PROLOG and to add certainty functions. Interfaces to conventional programming environments are available with some versions of PROLOG and to LISP.

OPS5

OPS5 (Official Production Systems 5) was developed at Carnegie-Mellon University. It was designed to support the construction of expert systems employing rules as the principal form of knowledge representation. It is a language in that it has its own syntax for encoding rules and data. It is a complete system since it has an on-board inference engine and a sophisticated pattern-matching algorithm. The Rete pattern-matching algorithm developed by Forgy and Shepard (1987) is elegant and fast. Because of its features, it is now used in many other expert system shells and special-purpose systems; implementations are found in C as well as LISP.

OPS5 also uses two-conflict resolution strategies to determine which rule of a set should fire first. LEX ("lexigraphic ordering") uses the following strategy for conflict resolution:

1. Refraction: Discard any instantiations that have already fired.
2. Recency: Pick the rule whose instantiations found in the antecedent are the freshest.
3. Specificity: Pick the rule that is the most selective, that is, has the most conditions in the antecedent.
4. Arbitrary: Pick any rule among those still tied.

MEA (means-ends) analysis, uses all of the conditions for LEX but splits the recency condition into two parts: recency of the first condition and recency of all other conditions in the antecedent.

OPS5 is written for implementation in several different LISP environments. It is available in the public domain and from commercial vendors who have added to the environment other features to aid in the development process, and it has been used successfully in a variety of large-scale expert systems. One of the most attractive features of OPS5 is its availability on both workstations and minicomputers. DP departments that already have a minicomputer capable of running one of the several dialects of LISP that OPS5 is compatible with can try some experimental work without a large out-of-pocket cost. On the other hand, OPS5 does not offer many of the sophisticated development tools that would come with a $10,000 workstation and $8,000 shell. Still, it is an option worth considering.

Conventional Languages

It should be apparent that LISP offers a powerful development environment, a database, and strong capabilities for symbolic processing. PROLOG offers an on-board inference engine, searching and control strategies, and a database. OPS5 offers a powerful tool for developing rule-based expert systems in a LISP environment on both workstations and minicomputers. Still, the functions required in most AI applications can be written in any conventional procedural language. C is the most widely used conventional language for AI applications.

The disadvantages of using C are obvious. It has no inference engine, no onboard database, and no backtracking algorithm. But there are appealing advantages. If you know the language already, you do not have to spend time learning LISP or PROLOG. The programs will be much faster and more compact and will not require huge amounts of expensive memory. There are a lot of C programmers and relatively few LISP and PROLOG programmers. This is particularly important to the DP manager who may have to support the software. If the target machine is a mainframe or minicomputer and the system is to be embedded in a larger one, then a conventional language like C is mandatory.

Even the disadvantages may not be serious if one uses a commercially available system that can convert a knowledge base to C and can provide the inference engine as well as other functions as part of a development environment. Several such systems are on the market.

The typical applications programmers should consider adding to their tool box the ability to embed a rule-based expert system in a conventionally developed program. All programmers know how to form a rudimentary rule base using the if-then construct, which exists in some form in most programming languages. Various parts of the knowledge base are scattered throughout the program in separately encoded "if statements."

The strategy used in an expert system is to gather up those pieces of knowledge that emulate what decision-makers do and put them together in a "rules procedure." Rules may also be gathered into rule sets (or multiple procedures) that will not be processed unless some condition is met. This has the effect of further structuring the program, facilitating the addition and alteration of rules, and making maintenance easier. Just building the knowledge base does not make it an expert system; an inference engine to control the firing of rules is needed and a forward-chaining approach is usually the simplest to implement.

In the discussion of OPS5, several criteria for conflict resolution were discussed. Each additional criterion adds to the complexity of the control process and should be considered in the long run. A simpler and cruder strategy is to order the rules in the order that they should fire (priority-based conflict resolution) and prevent the subsequent firing of any rule that would change the value of a variable set by an earlier firing.

A typical program would take data from a record (or complex record) in the database and/or from the operator and instantiate the variables used by the knowledge base. The rule procedure would be called, and new data would be inferred. Based on the conclusions reached, alternative actions would be undertaken by the balance of the program.

All of the caveats about developing expert systems in Chapter 4 apply equally well to conventional programming languages, but there is an advantage to working in an environment where the hardware and software capabilities are well known and access to the wealth of data in the organizational database is straightforward.

Selection

Expert systems can be implemented in any language. The choice depends on the task at hand. Arguments centering around what is the best AI language are not very useful if they are not conducted in the context of an application.

If the target environment does not support the language, the positive features of that language are of no value. If the language requires special equipment, such as a LISP machine or additional extended memory, and those resources are not forthcoming, that language will be rejected. If the system requires access to data from an external database and that access is not available in the language, the choice is narrowed. If there is no one available who can provide long-run support and maintenance for the application if written in the language, then look for another choice. If it is important to get a prototype up and running fast and rewrite for efficiency and speed later, the language chosen should be the one that lets the project be implemented the quickest.

UTILIZING ORGANIZATIONAL DATABASES

One of the most valuable resources that an organization has is its own database, and one of the reasons expert systems fail is that the interface or integration of the expert system and that database is incomplete or, worse, nonexistent. In this section the relationship between the database and the expert system is explored. Three areas are considered: (1) the relational database as a representation of knowledge, (2) using the database for setting certainty factors or probabilities, and (3) using the database in knowledge acquisition.

Relational Databases

A database designed to support criminal investigation has a number of relations, each representing exactly one type of information. A sample of these relations are:

1. Event.general: Contains one record for each event and a field for each attribute that applies to all events.

2. Event.crime: Contains one record for each event that is a crime and a field for each attribute that applies to all crimes.

3. Event.crime.specific: Contains one record for each crime of a specific type; burglary, for example, would be a separate relation from robbery and rape since the attributes are different for each type.

4. Arrest: Contains one record for each crime and criminal combination and attributes applying specifically to the arrest, including attributes about the arrest and attributes about the criminal that vary by time.

5. Property: Contains one record for each type of stolen property connected with a particular event.

6. Property.auto: Contains one record for each piece of property that is an automobile.

7. People: Contains one record for each person connected with an event (such as victim, witness, suspect, criminal).

8. People.criminal: Contains one record for each criminal and a field for each attribute that is constant.

Clearly the relational database can be used to represent and order knowledge if properly designed. The hierarchy and implicit inheritance is evident in the splitting of a general relation into several different relations where the attributes vary. In practice, the relational database requires a JOIN in order to access parts of the hierarchy.

Suppose we wanted to know what burglar is consistent with a set of facts about the case, (a backward chain). Given the facts that it was a nighttime entry, in an occupied residence, where the alarm was disabled, and only antiques were taken, perhaps we would begin by a PROJECT of all burglars who are not in jail and are assumed active. A JOIN of this subset with property would find antique thiefs, and a PROJECT would reduce the candidate set. Subsequent joins and projects would produce a subset that satisfies the required goal.

On the other hand, it is difficult to develop a way of inferring with the tools of the typical relational database. If the objective is to create a new relation called "profile," which contains part of the attributes of the criminal using forward chaining, there is no obvious way to do it. In a crude way, the relational database could be used directly to answer certain types of questions, but it would be quite clumsy in doing so. To overcome this problem, a number of commercial vendors are building rule-based systems on top of their relational databases and are employing natural language techniques used in AI as well.

To take advantage of these new technologies, database designers need to understand the basic concepts of AI. Additionally, they should also consider the relations and attributes that should be added to their organizational database to support the day-to-day work of members of the organization. All too often the organizational database design and content is driven by external reporting requirements (UCR), and not by the data required for operations.

The need to have the required data and structure available in the organization's database to support expert systems cannot be overemphasized. If the user of the expert system is required to answer a series of questions about data that they know exists in that database, the novelty of the system will soon wear off. Second, the results derived from the expert system may be part of a larger job. For example, most of the data in a CAD system are only indirectly related to the car or other resource to be dispatched. The results of the expert system need to be seen in the context of those other data. This is particularly important if mistakes are to be corrected and the expert system is to be validated, verified, and modified.

Certainty

One of the risks in building an expert system is that the rules derived in the knowledge acquisition process are wrong or produce results which are no better than a coin toss. This results, at least in part, from the inability of the expert or the knowledge engineer to reproduce the reasoning process by which the expert reaches any particular conclusion.

The organizational database may prove invaluable in evaluating the truth, or lack thereof, of any given rule. If both the data found in the antecedent of a rule and the consequent of the rule are contained in the database, it is straightforward to determine the accuracy of a rule based on experience. The analysis of each rule should show that the rule holds true an acceptable amount of the time (at least 70%), the rule is equally likely to produce a true result as a false result, or that the negated or opposite conclusion holds. Either the first or the last result could prove useful in building the final system. The "coin toss" conclusion would dictate discarding the rule.

The expert may be wrong for a number of reasons. The most obvious is that he or she is not an expert or that the knowledge engineering process failed. Another possibility is that the database covers cases outside the domain of the expert; that is, it is a local rule. Third, the database may reflect a different time period than the experience of the expert. It is not unusual to find changing conditions invalidating the past experience of experts. Finally, it is not unusual to find databases containing data generated from initial reports that subsequently are not updated by follow-up reports. If the initial data are generated by those less trained than the experts who gather the later data, contradictory outcomes could be found.

The other major benefit of conducting such an analysis both at the beginning and periodically during the expert system's life is the creation and modification of certainty factors. Certainty factors express the degree of confidence that the expert has in the truth of any specific rule. Such factors can be obtained subjectively (that is, personal opinion) or by analysis. Certainty factors are important to reasoning. If a conclusion is to be drawn on initial conditions that are known to be true, then the certainty factor assigned to the rule applies to the consequent of the rule. If the initial conditions were the result of previous inferences, then the certainty of the consequent of the second rule must be less than its assigned certainty.

The outcome of the rule-validation analysis produces as a side benefit a method for checking on the certainty factors assigned by the expert or by other methods. If these analyses are conducted periodically, the certainty factors on each rule can be updated, giving a more accurate assessment of the inferences of the system.

Knowledge Acquisition

The organizational database can be a rich source of rules to be used in the development of the expert system and its eventual modification. The process by which that is done is induction: creating general rules from specific instances. This procedure is risky to some degree because it can produce a false generalization, but it is the way many experts reach their conclusions in fields where there is not yet a strong theoretical framework. When we try to form rules by interrogating experts, we are in reality drawing from their collective experience (specific incidents) and asking them what conclusions have been drawn. If that experience is reflected in the database, it may be possible to develop rules directly from the data.

One of the problems noted earlier was that some of the data that the expert requires may not be recorded in the organization's database. If that can be said about the majority of the data used by the expert, then the current database will have to be augmented from paper files, if available, before proceeding. The organization's database should also be updated to add these new elements in the future.

The process of generating rules from existing data requires at least initial conditions. First, the goals or decisions that are the domain of the expert system must be known; second, the data representing those outcomes must have been recorded in the database. The outcome might be an attribute of an unobserved burglar. The task is to identify the antecedents that would allow one to draw the proper inference.

The first step is to determine the variables or attributes that could possibly play a role in producing the goal. The expert can assist greatly in this task, although the variables will be limited to the expert's specific set of experiences. There may be five variables that routinely affect the outcome, but the expert will give a laundry list of items that may have affected the outcome in unique cases. This is akin to the case where judges identify more than a hundred factors that affect sentencing decisions but the weight of most pale when compared to severity of the crime and previous criminal history.

Some statistical techniques, among them multiple discriminant analysis, cluster analysis, canonical correlation, probit, and logit, may be helpful in identifying variables. Ultimately, however, these procedures have limitations in assisting in the generation of rules because of the underlying mathematical models and the assumptions made by those models. A technique that is more of a tool for exploring data sets than for making statistical inferences is automatic interaction detection (AID).

AID, used in conjunction with a large data set and reasonably distributed data, produces a tree structure that divides the data set into a series of subgroups, all with the same characteristics. Given a group of burglars with an attribute level of experience (low, high), AID; attempts to split the group into two groups using one variable so that one group will have mostly low experienced and the other will have mostly highly experienced burglars. It examines each possible variable it could split on (method of entry, behavior in the residence, and so on) and finds that variable that, when split, will result in the widest difference between the two groups on the dependent or goal variable.

After making the first split, the algorithm will look at each split group and decide which has the greatest potential for further differentiating the overall group of burglars. This process continues until some limit on differentiation is reached, or the numbers of burglars in the current set of subgroups is too small to split further.

Each subgroup is equivalent to the consequent of a rule with a series of conditions; for example, entry by door, nonrandom search, occupied residence, and only sterling silverware taken imply experience. Some of the groups will be highly experienced, and others will have low experience. Rules are generated for ones that are homogeneous. The real difficulty is in deciding what do with those that are 60 percent experienced or 60 percent inexperienced. In most cases, the right approach is to exclude those groups when the variance increases too greatly. This essentially says that one should not infer characteristics when the result is random.

An examination of the tree structure produced by AID also gives a measure of the value of a split in that the difference between the means of the two groups most recently split is reported. A judgment can be made as to whether the result is sufficiently different to add to the complexity of the rule by adding another condition.

Induction techniques suggested in the AI literature and variations on them are available in some expert system shells and to some extent as stand-alone software. The concept learning system (CLS) and its descendant ID3 have been used successfully in single concept learning situations which can be represented as a decision tree. The AQ11 algorithm has also been used successfully. It is essentially a logic-based discriminant routine which does not suffer from some of the rigorous assumptions that can hamper the use of multiple discriminant analysis.

Rules generated in this way should be validated with the expert. Such rules might be combined with others derived from more traditional knowledge acquisition techniques that are submitted as a group to the expert for comment. The expert may find that the inclusion of one or more rules does not make sense in practice. Even if it predicts (and that may only be for this one sample), it is best to exclude that rule in subsequent trials.

Algorithms such as AID and AQ11 are not the only approach to development of rules from an existing database. If the variables to be used have been specified by the expert, the records can be ordered (sorted) along all of the candidate variables for conditions of the rule. Records that are alike will be adjacent. Assuming that the outcome is the same for identical records (and it may not be true), then some judgments can be made about how different the records can be before a different outcome is observed. The result will not always be perfect, as was observed for AID, but one of the basic tenets of heuristics is that the result of the rule should approximate truth, and the risk of being wrong is acceptable.

Not all variables are created equal in determining similarity. If two cases are alike on a characteristic and every case has that same value for the characteristic, the variable has no discriminatory value. On the other hand, if the two cases have the same value for a variable and relatively few other cases have that value, that variable will be relatively more important.

The importance of using the information found in the existing (or modified) database should not be discounted. In all likelihood, it will be the principal way of developing new rules and eliminating old ones as the system ages.

TOOLS

An expert system is composed of a number of components. Each component either has to be built or bought. The inference engine, which ultimately handles the reasoning processes of the system will, in almost all cases, be part of a commercial software package or shell. The knowledge base, which will hold the basic facts and rules of the system, has to be built and then is added to the shell housing the inference engine. The user interface, which determines how the expert system interacts with the expert system, must be built from scratch if a completely customized interface is needed, or it may utilize a menu-driven interface with modest customization provided by the shell. Finally, a database must be designed.

In a number of places in this book, we have suggested the use of a shell for at least prototyping the system. A shell contains at minimum an inference engine, a knowledge base with one or more forms of knowledge representation, and some kind of user interface (usually menu driven). Most also have an explanation facility, debugging systems, and other development tools. A few have knowledge acquisition tools and support for hyper-text.

Most of the shells run in a large PC environment. Some require true AI workstations such the TI Explorer or Symbolics. Some run only on the typical minicomputer, and others are a family with different versions of the shell for different target machines. A few run in the mainframe world.

The choice of a shell is heavily influenced by the target machine for the application, however, the inexperienced user would do well to consider a PC-based shell to gain some experience before investing in any of the larger machine systems or even the major PC shells.

Even among PC-based shells, there is a broad range. The high-end shells cost from $3,000 to $10,000. Most require an 80386 processor with a lot of disk and memory, which brings the hardware cost to nearly $10,000. Among these systems are Goldworks by Gold Hill Computers, KEE by Intellicorp, Personal Consultant Plus by Texas Instruments, KES by Software A&E, NEXPERT by Neuron Data, M1 by Teknowledge Inc., GURU by MDBS Inc., and ART by Inference Corp. These are full-service shells and in most cases have other versions for workstations and minicomputers. There is a middle ground with products in the $500 to $1,500 price range. These include products such as Expert-Ease by Perrone and Associates, ESP by Expert Systems International, KDS3+ by KDS Corp,

FUSION by 1ST Class Expert Systems, Exsys Professional by EXSYS Inc., and Level 5 by Information Builders. Under $500 we find products such as the Personal Consultant by Texas Instruments, EXSYS by EXSYS Inc, VP-Expert by Paperback Publishing, Insight2+ by Level5, and KnowledgePro by Knowledge Garden.

There is a reason for the price differential. It may be because of a limitation of the inference engine (only forward or only backward chaining). It may reflect the lack of an explanation facility or user interface development capabilities. Rules may be the only form of knowledge representation, or the number of rules may be limited. Still, the cost may represent features that are not needed at this time or features that require a level of expertise not found on current staff. In the early stages, consider one of the lower-cost shells that supports rules and frames, uses forward and backward chaining, and has a good debugging capability. Once you are familiar with the logic and procedures of expert systems and begin to be limited by the shell, that is the time to look at the marketplace again.

For those interested in PROLOG, Borland's Turbo PROLOG is a good place to start, although it may be a dead-end product. Full-featured PROLOGs are supplied by companies such as ARITY, Cogent Software, and Expert Systems. C programmers may wish to use CXPERT by Software Plus or CLIPS, which was developed by NASA and is distributed by COSMIC at the University of Georgia.

The marketplace for AI-related software is exploding, and the capabilities of the general-purpose shells are too. (See "Vendors" at the end of this book.) It pays to look around and to read reviews in the AI magazines.

7

CASE STUDY OF THE BALTIMORE COUNTY POLICE DEPARTMENT'S EXPERT SYSTEM

The BCPD is home to the first operational expert system developed for a local law enforcement agency in the United States. Supported by a National Institute of Justice grant to the Jefferson Institute for Justice Studies, AI system technology was applied to residential burglaries. This expert system simulates the thought processes of experienced detectives. It uses their knowledge to make inferences about the identity of likely suspects based on the behavioral fingerprints they leave at the scene of a residential burglary.

Law enforcement practitioners must understand and recognize the impact these systems have on their procedures and resources, for these effects play a determining role in the success of the operation and its deployment in the field. They also have implications for a police department's training programs and report writing procedures.

This case study is provided to give law enforcement officials a background to the use of expert systems as they are applied to a specific crime problem, and to describe the steps that need to be taken in developing a system. It is presented in chronological order to add a time dimension to the work undertaken on this project.

This case study was excerpted from "Building an Expert System for the Baltimore County Police Department", a final report submitted by the Jefferson Institute for Justice Studies to the National Institute for Justice, under the terms of grant number 87-IJ-CX-0019.

BACKGROUND

The BCPD's residential burglary expert system is the outgrowth of a pattern-matching project conducted jointly by the Devon and Cornwall Constabulary in Exeter, England, and Robert Lucas of the Savant Research Centre at Coventry Polytechnic, England. The operational research division of the Devon and Cornwall Constabulary (D&CC) designed and developed a comprehensive, integrated crime analysis program that incorporated the best practices of policing into all aspects of law enforcement, from report writing using laptop computers to crime analysis. Included in this comprehensive effort were plans to use expert systems to aid in the solution of residential burglaries. This comprehensive program had been under development for about eight years before a transfer of the expert system portion to other jurisdictions was contemplated.

In October 1986, the Jefferson Institute for Justice Studies began to explore the possibility of developing an expert system based on the experience of the D&CC's work in the area of residential burglaries. The institute was looking for a progressive police department with strong ties to the federal criminal justice research community and one with a solid reputation among local law enforcement agencies to house this effort. The BCPD met these criteria and had a distinct advantage over other potential sites because of its proximity to the Washington, D.C. area, home of the National Institute of Justice and the Jefferson Institute for Justice Studies.

In historical context, 4 November 1986 is a significant date because it represents the decision to develop the expert system in the United States. Representatives from the BCPD and the D&CC met to exchange information on the operations of each respective burglary and crime analysis units. By the end of November 1986, the BCPD had agreed in principle to become the development site.

In the spring of 1987, the National Institute of Justice funded a project designed to capitalize on the existing developmental effort at the D&CC. Its primary objective was to transfer the technical knowledge and experience from England to a local law enforcement agency in the United States. The BCPD agreed to become the test site for the transfer. The project began in May 1987 when the National Institute of Justice formally awarded a grant to the Jefferson Institute to accomplish this task. The prototype system was in place in

Baltimore County in April 1988, slightly ahead of its scheduled implementation date.

THE BCPD'S EXPERT SYSTEM FOR RESIDENTIAL BURGLARIES

The BCPD's expert system simulates the thinking patterns of the most experienced burglary detectives in the department. Their knowledge about the investigation and solution of residential burglaries is extracted, and rephrased as rules that take the form of if-then statements. For example, one BCPD rule is, "If the medicine cabinet was searched, then the suspect is a drug abuser".

Rules are derived from the inferences detectives make about the identity of the burglar. They stem from the characteristics of the burglary and the behavior of the suspect at the scene of the crime. Since not all rules are true all the time, attached to each rule is a certainty value or probability that represents the likelihood of its' occurring. In the above example, the detectives assigned a value of .90 to the rule. This means that in one case out of ten, the rule would not apply.

The output of the expert system is similar to the output produced from automated fingerprint identification systems. The system provides a list of suspects with an associated probability of their being the offender. If no suspect is found, the system has the ability to produce a profile of the suspect.

Project Work Steps

There are many steps between the decision to implement an expert system and its actual operation. Here we describe the significant ones. We briefly document the experiences of the BCPD in setting up the residential burglary expert system, and highlight material events and major milestones.

The development of the expert system was under the direction of the Jefferson Institute. It involved extensive scheduling and coordination among four entities: BCPD, D&CC, the Jefferson Institute, and Edward Ratledge at the University of Delaware. Project tasks were divided between program activities, and computer systems work. The programmatic work under the direction on the Jefferson Institute, included rules development, database development, and program implementation. The computer systems work was directed and conducted by Ed Ratledge. It included system design, programming, implementation on site, training on site, testing and debugging, and technical assistance.

Step 1: Designation of Project Team. Consistent with their internal project management structure, the BCPD formed a project team. The Criminal Investigation Division commander was responsible for operational functions and for the direction and coordination of various special projects, including this one. Day-to-day project coordination rested with the commander of the Crimes against Property section.

Having an operational commanding officer coordinate all of the activities was especially suitable for this project. The expert system is a detective-based system, built by them and for them. Although expert system technology is sophisticated in design and advanced in technique, it still demands a major and continuing participatory role by the operational detectives.

In April 1987, the project team assigned Detective Bruce Magladry to the expert system project on a full-time basis. Although acting in a full-time capacity, the detective continued to work some investigations and attended court during the initial stages of the project.

Step 2: Jurisdictional Comparison of Burglaries and Burglars. After designation of the project team, the BCPD sent three crime investigative representatives to Exeter, England. They determined the extent to which the D&CC and English police practices in solving residential burglaries differed from U.S. practices and identified differences due to the nature and characteristics of burglars and burglaries in Exeter. Working with representatives from the D&CC, they examined policing practices and burglary crime scenes and exchanged information on police operations and crime analysis systems. A brief report highlighting these differences was prepared by this team for the Jefferson Institute and Ed Ratledge in preparation for the rules meeting in June 1987.

Step 3: Rules Meeting at BCPD Training Academy. The first step in building an expert system is to develop the rules that drive the expert system. This is done in a series of steps. The first is taken at a rules meeting. The primary purpose of this meeting is to extract knowledge from BCPD detectives that would subsequently be rephrased into a set of rules. Detectives Magladry and Robert Hardester were designated as lead detectives. They were responsible for providing guidance about the design of the workshops and interpreting the results of the rules meeting to the researchers. A two-day meeting with twelve experienced burglary detectives and six others with related experience (including crime lab technicians) was held on 25 and 26 June 1987.

The eighteen participants were divided into small work groups, led by experienced facilitators to extract the knowledge from the detectives. To structure the discussion, descriptive information on the burglary and the burglar was categorized to describe the elements of the offense. The categories designated were:

* characteristics of residence and the environment
* type of entry
* type and extent of search
* property taken/not taken
* behavior at the scene
* transportation

The participants were asked to identify and specify relationships that exist within each category and between other categories. Through this process, the detectives were able to articulate the characteristics of the offender given these attributes of the crime scene.

As a result of this session, 397 statements were made about residential burglaries. These statements reflected what detectives said about the various categories and their interrelationships and indicated how the detectives made inferences about the crime scene and the likely suspect.

In order to obtain a measure of reliability for these statements, forty-three detectives were asked to review them and state whether they agreed or disagreed with each statement, using a five-level Likert scale. The tabulation of these ratings indicated the overall confidence the detectives had in the statements made by the group. Statements that engendered 66 percent or more disagreement among the detectives were initially rejected.

Step 4: Attachment of Certainty Values to Rules. In the real world, one estimates the probability that a rule is true based on its frequency of occurrence. For example, if eight out of ten entries by body force are done by inexperienced youths, the probability of that rule is .80. However, since many of the rules could not be statistically verified until a large database was produced, the initial assignment of probabilities had to be based on alternative means. They were initially calculated in two ways: using the probabilities obtained from the distributions of the Likert-scale evaluations and having the lead detectives review all the rules and readjust values for those that had wide variation in agreement or were not consistent with their experience.

Step 5: Formulation of Rule Base. The conversion process from statements into rules was guided by the premise that rules should make inferences about who would be the most likely offender given a particular set of circumstances or M.O. In August 1987, meetings between the Jefferson Institute and the BCPD were held to convert the statements into rules for the expert system.

Some of the statements were not rules but had significant value for an investigators' training course. For example, the statement that "burglars will not take silver and jewelry unless they have fences or a means of disposal" does not necessarily identify the suspect but gives the detective leads as to where to look for the stolen property. These statements were saved and were subsequently used, along with the rules, as a basis for developing an investigators' training course.

Step 6: Creation of the Data Collection Form. The rules defined what data elements had to be collected. If, for example, a rule stated that "if the house is protected by an alarm system, then the suspect is experienced," then *alarm system* would have to be a data element on the incident report. The inclusion of data elements on the form was justified simply: each relates to a specific inference made by detectives about the suspect and each could be tied to one or more rules.

At the time, BCPD was collecting only a small percentage of data elements that the rules demanded. A comparison of data elements collected on BCPD Form 296 (standard incident M.O., the crime analysis form completed for all cases) showed that much of the information being collected was not operationally useful for the detectives in solving residential burglaries. In fact, a comparison of the data elements on Form 296 with those needed by the expert system indicated that only 37 percent of the data items required would support the information needed by the rules.

In September 1987, meetings were held between the Jefferson Institute and the BCPD to design the initial data collection form. It was also decided that this form would stand alone until the system was completed, at which time BCPD could decide whether to integrate it into the department's reporting system or leave it independent.

Step 7: Data Collection Procedures. After the form was designed, procedures for data collection were established. Because the form collected information about all aspects of the burglary in a checklist format, its value was immediately recognized by the crime lab road technicians in Baltimore County who volunteered to collect the crime scene data for the expert system, replacing their old narrative form with this one. These technicians visited all residential burglary crime scenes (except domestic incidents and out buildings that were excluded from the expert system). The information they collected at the scene was forwarded daily to the Crime Analysis Unit.

Initially, the data collection forms were forwarded to Edward Ratledge, the systems engineer who was working parallel with these program activities on the technical design and development features of the expert system. Later the forms were inputted directly into the computer by detective personnel. Today, each incident report form takes the detectives less than thirty seconds to input.

Step 8: Building a Database from Closed-Case Data. The success of the expert system depends on the number of active residential burglars in the database. One cannot identify likely suspects if their records are not included in the system. Thus, it was important to build a database of closed cases that contained suspect and behavioral information as quickly as possible.

As a first step, each detective was asked to complete an expert system form for ten cases that he or she had cleared by an arrest. This process ensured that a name was attached to the M.O. of a burglary and that other demographic data such as age, race, and sex were captured. It produced an immediate file of about three hundred closed cases.

In some cases, it was not possible to reconstruct all the data elements needed by the expert system. Most notably absent was the environmental information such as type of housing, access to public transportation, or whether entrances were visibly obscured. The system, however, was designed to accept cases with missing data. It merely produced identifications of likely suspects with a reduced level of certainty.

Second, information contained on the BCPD Data Base III system was downloaded to the expert system. About 3,000 records were entered into the system. This defined the universe of known, arrested burglars and unsolved cases. However, it was not especially useful to the inferencing part of the system since only a small percentage of the data elements needed by the system were available from this set.

Finally, through the Crime Analysis Unit's known offender system, burglars being released from the state's Division of Corrections were identified. The burglary detectives were asked to reconstruct the old cases cleared by the offender and enter these data into the system.

Step 9: Systems Design and Programming. In September and October 1987, the crucial differences in the direction of the systems development between D&CC and BCPD became apparent. The D&CC pattern-matching system was developed on a VAX using PROLOG. (It is currently being redesigned to use high-performance AI workstations.) The development equipment and environment costs associated with their system were not cost-effective for BCPD and other local U.S. law enforcement agencies. Consequently the BCPD design was redeveloped to a PC environment using an 80386-based machine and Gold Works marketed and licensed by Gold Hill Products.

By January 1988, much of the programming for the expert system was completed. Test data were sent from BCPD to debug the system and to begin initial implementation of the on-line database. Screens for the system were created from the data elements incorporated on the expert system form.

Step 10: Data Entry Procedures and Systems Operations. Detective Donald Byrd from the Crime Analysis Unit was assigned to the expert system. He worked with the systems engineer in debugging, and developing editing and validation procedures for the system. It was agreed in December 1987 that the Crime Analysis Unit would begin to input data into the system and be responsible for their completeness and accuracy.

Step 11: Public Documentation. Spokespersons were selected by BCPD to address media questions about the project and to prepare public information reports on an as-needed basis. The designations were based on rank and level of responsibility to the project.

The BCPD project team did not agree on whether the expert system should be given general publicity. Some felt that the success of the system would be jeopardized if burglars had knowledge of the power of the technology. They argued that residential burglars would change their behavioral patterns if they knew that their particular methods could lead to an arrest. Others disagreed. It was finally agreed that information on the expert system would be dispersed by BCPD through the conduit of police networks.

Step 12: Training of Detectives. In January 1988, the project team designated Detective Byrd as coordinator for the training and implementation of expert systems. Their selection criteria were based on persons who enjoy computers and the technology that makes them work, who were willing to put in the extra time and effort to ensure the success of the expert system, and who could act as the primary contact person with the systems engineer and the detectives. To prepare him further, Detective Byrd was sent to a Goldworks training course in Boston.

Step 13: Running the Expert System in Test Mode. The expert system was delivered to the BCPD in April 1988 to run in test mode. During this phase, the systems designer and the detective interacted frequently as the debugging phase was entered.

The property crimes detectives were trained by Detective Byrd in the use of the system beginning in April 1988. Making the detectives feel comfortable interacting with the expert system is vital to its success. They were taught all the procedures from logging on, to matching suspects or incidents to the database, to the adjustments to the rules. The training was scheduled over the detectives' workdays.

Step 14: Operating Procedures for Utilization. The development of an operations manual was the final step in the development of the BCPD expert system. This manual describes all the procedures necessary to operate the expert system. It details steps including how to fill out the expert system form, data entry instructions, and usage techniques for new detectives unfamiliar with the system. The manual is available to other police departments interested in utilizing expert systems.

Costs and Program Implications

Although the expert system was developed with National Institute of Justice funds at little cost to BCPD in equipment and software, it is not free to other jurisdictions.

The BCPD residential burglary expert system operates on a COMPAQ 386 with 10 megabytes of memory and 6 megabytes of hard disk. An additional 9 megabytes of memory were purchased for the system. The cost for this configuration is about $11,000. A printer costs about $200.

The expert system utilizes LISP shells. Some of the software used in the system is licensed. This includes Gold

Works, LISP, and the programming language C. The costs for these licenses are about $6,000.

Included also as a cost are the maintenance contracts on the hardware and software, which will average about $3,000 annually. Computer supplies should increase the annual cost by another $1,500.

The BCPD costs for the equipment were as follows:

Hardware
Compaq 386: $6,800
Additional memory(9 megabytes): $4,050
Hardware maintenance contract: $1,500

Software
Goldworks LISP shell: $5,000
D Base and C program: $700
Software maintenance contract: $800

Computer Supplies
Computer paper: $1,000
Floppy disks: $200
Miscellaneous supplies: $300

Training
Goldworks Software Training Course: $1,000
Total costs:　　$21,350
Annual costs: $ 3,800

Reflections and Insights

If expert systems are to work in a detective environment, three areas need special attention. One is fairly straightforward: building a database of suspects. The second is operationally more subtle: integrating the expert system with other complementary crime-solving procedures. And the third looks to the problems created by multiple users. Each of these areas has to be given consideration as part of this application.

BUILDING A DATABASE OF SUSPECTS

An expert system cannot be productive until a sufficient number of residential burglars and burglaries is entered into the database. Adding offense data should not be difficult if the department maintains automated files. This information establishes the universe of solved and unsolved offenses, although it will be incomplete (not containing all the required data elements). However, the newly-designated burglary reports will contain all the required information. Crime scene data are inputted into the system as they are reported by the collectors-- crime lab technicians, patrol officers, and others.

There are basically two sources for offense information: patrol and crime lab technicians. BCPD chose to use crime lab road technicians because there were only fourteen of them; they responded to all residential burglaries (except domestic related), and they liked the form needed by the expert system better than the narrative one they were using. This selection had the obvious advantage of centralizing the data collection effort and increasing the quality of the reports because of this and the small number of collectors.

Other jurisdictions may use patrol officers to collect burglary information. In this case, the department needs to establish a training mechanism and provide strong monitoring and review controls. These controls should be installed at the precinct level, others by crime analysis, and even more at the time of data input to the system.

Since arrest rates are traditionally low, one cannot assume that a "go-forward" approach for arrestees will produce a large database in a reasonable amount of time. Therefore, there has to be a reconstruction effort. This means that the department will have to devise ways for doing this. The techniques used in BCPD are important, but others should also be considered. The reconstruction effort will have to be tailored to each jurisdiction since it depends on such factors as level and extent of automation, location and condition of manual record-keeping systems, and personnel available to perform the task. All police departments should consider the time and resources it will take to go back into closed cases and retrieve information for the expert system database before making the decision to implement this technology.

Since the expert system produces behavioral fingerprints of burglars, it becomes more reliable as the number of cases connected to the burglar increases. Thus, the priority for reconstruction should be the most active burglars in the community and then all the cases associated with the burglar, not just the latest ones. The expert system has the ability to degrade the M.O.s of old offenses and give more weight to newer ones. It performs better with the greatest number of incidents associated with the offender than with the least number.

INTEGRATION WITH OTHER DETECTIVE TOOLS

A residential burglary expert system works best when is complemented by other investigative resources and procedures. Of the tools available to detectives, information is the most important. This is especially true in residential burglary cases where the physical evidence is often negligible.

In one sense, we can think of the expert system as an extension of the crime analysis function into an operational environment. This is because, like crime analysis, many sources of information are used in tandem to reach certain conclusions about the known identity of the suspect.

In Baltimore County, these sources of information include: a record of stolen and recovered property; an automated fingerprint identification system (PRINTRAK) that contains the known prints of 306,000 previously arrested suspects; a central records department for criminal histories; and an automated system, POSSE, which records every contact of the police with citizenry, whether criminal or noncriminal. Additionally. the Crime Analysis Unit in Baltimore County gathers information from burglary reports and arranges that information by computer in an effort to discern patterns and trends. Finally, the department uses MCI as part of its investigative procedures. All of these manual and automated systems operate independently but work interactively with the expert system to provide detectives with the maximum amount of information and support for their case clearance efforts.

The residential burglary expert system is not a supersleuth or a Sherlock Holmes but rather a tireless and invaluable detective's assistant who uses every resource available to help solve crimes.

ACCESS FOR MULTIPLE USERS

Currently the residential burglary expert system supports a single user on a stand-alone machine. This situation creates problems for BCPD and other departments whose burglary detail is decentralized or dispersed and whose computer sits at central headquarters. The success of the system is clearly dependent on its use by detectives; thus, obstacles to access are important concerns.

There are a number of solutions. The first is to designate a lead detective for each area or region who coordinates detectives' inquiries at the central location. This may be awkward but can help in the short run. Another is to install remote terminals at the various locations that can be accessed but cannot be updated. Here the cost of the terminals needs to be considered. A long-term solution rests in converting the system to a UNIX multi-user environment. In a UNIX environment, police departments with decentralized operations are able to access the expert system from various precincts in the jurisdiction through linked computer networks and update the files as needed. This option and ones similar to it are being explored by Ed Ratledge. One can expect that this problem may be reduced as the system technology advances; for the present time, however, it is an issue that should be addressed by the department.

If there is one final reflection to be made about this project, it is that the speed with which systems advance and progress will probably make this particular application in Baltimore County obsolete by the time this book is published. Thus, once embarked upon this adventure, it is necessary to keep abreast of updates and improvements that tend to decrease in cost as they increase in efficiency.

APPENDIX A:
TECHNICAL TERMS
AND GLOSSARY

A*. An algorithm used in searching which attempts to find an optimum solution in the shortest time.

AFIS. Automated fingerprint identification system

Agenda. A prioritized list of pending activities. In the context of expert systems, this might be a list of all possible rules that might be fired in the next pass.

AI. Artificial intelligence.

AID. Automatic interaction detection.

AIMS. Arson information management system.

Algorithm. A step-by-step procedure for solving a problem.

Analogical reasoning. A procedure for drawing conclusions about a problem by analyzing a model or analog of it.

Analogy. A statement that shows the similarities between two things along some dimension.

AND/OR tree. A method of graphically representing the solution of a problem by breaking it up into a set of smaller problems.

Antecedent. The condition in the "if" part of a rule.

Arc. The lines connecting intersections in a search tree.

Architecture. The framework or structure of a computer or a piece of software.

Argument. A value or variable which is provided as input to a function or procedure.

Array. A matrix of symbols or numbers.

ART or *Automated Reasoning Tool*. Developed by the Inference Corp.

Artificial Intelligence. The part of computer science which studies how to use computers to simulate human mental processes.

Atomatic programming. An area in the field of artificial intelligence which deals with the ability to create new software. It is found particularly in LISP since LISP programs can also be used as input.

AVL. Automatic vehicle location.

AVM. Automated vehicle monitoring.

Backward chaining. A technique used in searching where one starts with the desired final outcome, and works backward to see if the data is consistent with that outcome.

BCPD. Baltimore County Police Department.

Best first. A search technique which uses both depth and breadth first strategies to find the best path.

BJA. Bureau of Justice Assistance.

Blind search. A search technique(s) that does not attempt to speed up or simplify the search process using rules of thumb.

Breadth first. A search strategy where all of the nodes on one level of the search tree are examined before going deeper in a tree.

C. A popular third generation programming language widely used by all levels of machines for both applications and systems programming.

CAD. Computer-aided dispatch.

CAI. Computer-assisted instruction.

CBT. Computer-based training.

Certainty. A measure of the confidence given by a user or expert system as to the validity of a proposition or rule.

Certainty factor. A number usually assigned to the consequent of a rule which suggests the degree of confidence one should have in that rule.

Children. Nodes in a search tree which are derived from a parent. Children frames of parents may inherit characteristics.

Cognition. The mental process of knowing or having knowledge.

Cognitive science. An interdisciplinary science concerned with all aspects of modelling and understanding how humans think and how to use computers in that research.

Combinatorial explosion. A situation that occurs in searching when a very large number of possible alternatives exist, all of which must be searched in order to find the goal. At some point, the time of the search becomes impossibly long and blind search must be rejected.

Common LISP. A version of the LISP programming language.

Computer vision. A part of AI research that seeks to simulate human vision for use in robots or other applications.

Confidence factor. A number or system of numbers indicating the certainty or confidence we have in a specific fact, statement or piece of evidence. The degree of truthfulness or belief we have in our information or knowledge. A method of dealing with uncertainty in production rule systems. Not the same as probability.

Consequent. The result found in the "then" part of a rule.

Control strategy. A method used in searching a state space (e.g., depth first etc.).

COPE. Citizen-oriented police enforcement.

CPU. Central Processing Unit. That portion of the computer that actually controls the computer and executes instructions.

CRT. Cathode-ray tube.

Data driven. A kind of strategy used in searching. Data driven reasoning is forward-chaining.

DBMS. Data Base Management Systems. It is a major piece of software that allows the separation of database functions from the application.

DEA. Drug Enforcement Agency.

D&CC. Devon and Cornwall Constabulary.

Deductive reasoning. Reasoning from the general to the specific. Typically used to argue a specific outcome based on general principles or theories.

Default value. A value given to a variable if no other value is defined. Slots in frames typically have default values.

Dependency. A relation between the antecedents and corresponding consequents produced as a result of firing a rule. Typically used in expert system to allow the retraction of consequents whose antecedents are no longer true.

Depth first. A search procedure which follows each branch of a tree to its termination point before moving to any other candidate branch.

Domain. A field of knowledge.

DP. Data processing.

ELIZA. A program developed at MIT which simulates a psychiatrist. It is an application of the natural language area of artificial intelligence.

Embedded system. AI software built into another larger piece of software.

EMS. Emergency medical service

EMYCIN. A shell of the widely known MYCIN expert system which can be used to develop new systems.

EPA. Environmental Protection Agency

Environment. A software and hardware development facility provided to assist the developer in the creation of new software.

Expert system. A computer system which uses knowledge derived from experts to simulate the behavior of human beings that normally would require years of experience and/or training.

Expert system shell. A tool designed to simplify the development of an expert system. It will usually include at least an inference engine and methods of knowledge representation.

Explanation Facility. The ability to justify to the user the reasons behind any particular action.

Fact. A data item which is accepted as true.

FBI. Federal Bureau of Investigation.

Fifth generation. The term used by the Japanese to refer to their attempt to leapfrog current software development processes using techniques of artificial intelligence.

Fire. The process of asserting the consequent of a rule.

Forward-chaining. A search strategy primarily used in rule-based systems where conclusions are drawn starting with the known facts and attempt to find a goal.

Fourth generation language. A non-procedural language usually found in a DBMS used to facilitate the creation of applications.

Frame. A knowledge representation method that associates one or more attribute, characteristic or property called slots with a particular object, event or action.

Franz LISP. Another version of the LISP programming language.

Front-end. Hardware or software that provides functions to aid in the use of another piece of hardware or software.

Function. In software, typically a small self-contained piece of programming that is designed to do a single thing.

Fuzzy reasoning. A method of dealing with inexact or imprecise information by specifying not one value but a set of values with their associated probabilities.

Garbage collection. In LISP based machines largely, the process of clearing memory of unneeded data so that new data can be added.

Generate and test. A problem-solving method.

Goal driven. A method of reasoning that starts with the goal or conclusion and works backward through the a knowledge base searching for a path in which the data is consistent with the goal.

Heuristic. The use of empirical knowledge to aid in problem-solving.

Heuristic rule. A rule of thumb which is right most of the time that helps in the speedier solution of a problem.

Hierarchy. Knowledge or information organized into successive layers.

Hypothesis. A proposition used as the basis for argument, discussion or reasoning.

IF-THEN. The form of the rules used in many expert systems.

Inductive reasoning. Reasoning from the specific to the general.

Inference. The process of drawing a conclusion from an initial set of facts.

Inference engine. That part of an expert system that actually performs the reasoning process by analyzing the knowledge base and firing rules using some control strategy.

Inheritance. The method by which one object assumes the characteristics of its parent.

Instantiation. The process of assigning a specific value to a particular "instance" of that variable.

Intelligence. The ability to acquire knowledge and then to apply it.

Interface. A piece of hardware or software that links two points of a system.

IRS. Internal Revenue Service.

Knowledge. Facts, beliefs and heuristics.

Knowledge acquisition. The extraction of knowledge, usually from experts.

Knowledge base. A collection of facts, data, rules, and inferences, organized using one or more methods of knowledge representation. The inclusion of rules and other information about a domain are an extension to the typical database.

Knowledge-based systems. Systems that depend on their knowledge base to perform the task required of the system.

Knowledge engineer. A person who is an expert in knowledge acquisition and knowledge representation. The builder of the knowledge base.

Knowledge engineering. The process through which expert systems and other knowledge based systems are built.

Knowledge representation. The structural methods by which knowledge is organized to support the solution of the problem of interest.

Language. A set of words and symbols with a particular syntax or structure used in communicating with men and machines.

Learning. The process by which we gain new knowledge, discard disproven theory, and modify current knowledge.

LEX. Lexigraphic ordering.

LISP (List Processor). The most common programming language used in building artificial intelligence applications. It is oriented toward the processing of symbols.

LISP machine. A computer specifically designed to support the LISP programming environment.

List. A series of symbols contained within parentheses. It is the form that the LISP programming language is designed to manipulate.

Logic. A mathematical reasoning process developed for the purpose of inferring unobserved information from facts.

MCI. Managing criminal investigations.

MDC. Mobile digital communications.

Means-ends analysis. One of several methods for controlling the search process.

Menu. Typically a list of options presented to a user which describes the alternative activities available for the user to pursue.

Metaknowledge. Knowledge that tells about how other knowledge is to be used or interpreted.

Metarule. A rule that states how other rules should operate.

Minimax. A search procedure typically used in the playing of games.

MIS. Management information systems.

MO. Modus operandi.

MYCIN. Probably the first usable expert system. A rule-based expert system that helps doctors to diagnose particular types of infection and to select among treatment alternatives.

Natural language. An area of explanation for AI scientists concerned primarily with understanding the content of language using machines.

Natural language interface. That portion of a piece of software which endeavors to allow the user to enter unstructured commands but still understand what is to be done.

Natural language processing. The process by which the computer understands what it has been asked to do.

NCVAC. National Center for the Analysis of Violent Crime.

NIH. Not invented here.

Nodes. The different states that one finds within a search tree.

Object-oriented programming. The programming method by which data and procedures are gathered together in objects and those objects react when messages are passed to them.

Operating system. The piece of software that enables the various components of a computer to do useful work.

OPS. A rule-based programming language developed at Carnegie Mellon University designed to implement expert systems.

OPS5. Official Production Systems 5. A variant of the OPS programming language.

Paradigm. A model.

Parsing. The process of separating a line of input to a computer into a series of tokens or words.

Path. A route through a search tree.

PATRIC. Pattern recognition and information corrections.

Pattern. A known series of steps or symbols usually associated with some goal.

Pattern-matching. The process of recognizing an input pattern by matching it to other patterns which are generally stored. A match will generally cause some action to be taken.

Predicate. A statement about the relationship between an object and its domain. Usually found in connection with reasoning systems using predicate logic.

Predicate calculus. A system of reasoning used in AI programs, in particular, PROLOG, to indicate relationships among data items.

Primitive. A fixed or built-in function found in a computer language.

Probability. The likelihood of the occurrence of a specific event. Used in some rule based system to deal with uncertainty.

Problem-solving. The process by which a solution to a problem is found. Most expert systems are essentially problem solvers.

Procedure. A module found in a computer program that executes a specific task. Most programs are a bundle of distinct procedures.

Production rule. See *Rule.*

Production system. The method of problem solving that expresses its knowledge base in the form of rules.

PROLOG. PROgramming in LOGic. A widespread language which employs predicate logic as the method of problem solving.

PROMIS. Prosecutor's management information system.

Propositional calculus. A system used in logic for reasoning about known facts.

PROSPECTOR. An expert system designed to find ore deposits from using rules derived from an expert geologist.

Real time computing. Processing that occurs for all practical purposes instantaneously (e.g. shuttle navigation).

Reasoning. The process of drawing conclusions using facts, and other knowledge.

Recursive. Any operation that is defined in terms of itself.

RICO. Racketeer Influenced and Corrupt Organizations.

Robotics. That area of artificial intelligence that is concerned with using machines to simulate the actions that a human would take when doing a particular task.

Root node. The starting state in a search tree.

Rule. A method of knowledge representation which expresses knowledge in terms of a condition (If __) and an action (Then __)

Rule-based program. Any program that uses rules as its principal method of knowledge representation and is designed to solve problems.

Rule of thumb. A technique employed by most humans to simplify or speed up a search for solutions.

Ruleset. A collection of rules usually formed to be triggered by a meta-rule.

Scenario. A description of an imaginary or hypothetical situation.

Schema. A method of knowledge representation.

Scripts. A form of schema which employs descriptions of commonly occurring situations or modes of behavior.

Search. The process by which goals are found.

Search space. The space which contains all possible states that one might attain and hopefully the desired goal.

Search tree. A map of the search space which must be traversed to reach a goal.

Semantic network. A method of knowledge representation which graphically represents objects and the links between objects.

Shell. A software development environment which contains the tools necessary for constructing an expert system. Shells usually include an inference engine, methods of knowledge representation, and often knowledge acquisition tools.

Simulation. The process of having a computer mimic or imitate some physical or social system. Studying or designing a system or process by having the computer duplicate it.

Slot. The basic component of a frame. It may consist of a value, a default, constraints, and may have procedures associated with it.

Software. A set of instructions written in a language understood by a computer, designed to give a particular outcome.

SOP. Standard operating proceedure.

SRI. Standard Research Institute.

SUSCOM. Sussex County Communications Center.

Symbol. Something that represents something else. Usually used as a shorthand method of expressing complex ideas or objects.

Symbolic computing. Computing using symbols instead of numbers with the general methodology being a reasoning process.

Template. A known pattern which is matched to other patterns in the search process.

Tree. A graphical representation of a search space.

Unification. The process employed in PROLOG which is equivalent to instantiation in LISP whereby actual values are substituted in a pattern in order to find a match.

User interface. That portion of a computer program that is seen by the user. It typically allows the user to control its major functions and to provide input and output.

VICAP. Violent Criminal Apprehension Program.

Workstation. A high powered, usually single-user computer dedicated to a specific application such as computer-aided design with special features designed to assist that particular application.

ZetaLISP. Another version of the LISP programming language found on particular AI work stations.

APPENDIX B:
EXPERT SYSTEM VENDORS
AND AI PUBLICATIONS

Abacus Programming Corp.
14545 Victory Boulevard
Van Nuys, California 91411
(818) 785-8000
ESI

ADS: $7,000 for PCs, $60,000-$70,000 for mainframes, depending on operating system
AION Corp.
101 University Avenue
Palo Alto, California 94301
(415) 328-9595
Available for the IBM PC/XT/AT and compatibles, PS/2, and IBM mainframes. Runs under OS/2, MS-DOS, MVS/TSO, CICS, VM/CMS, and MVS/XA. Designed for large-scale corporate applications. Supports direct access to QSAM, VSAM, DL/1, DB2, and SQL/DS. Products developed under ADS on the PC can be easily ported to mainframes.

ALEX System $675
Harris and Hall Associates
P.O. Box 1900
Port Angeles, Washington 98362
(800) 433-1983, (206) 457-4907
Available for any machine that can use Smalltalk/V. Runs in Smalltalk environment. Allows programmers to develop object-oriented expert systems.

Arity Expert: $295
Arity Corp.
29 Domino Drive
Concord, Massachusetts 01742
(508) 371-1243

Available for the PC/XT/AT, PS/2, and compatibles. Runs under MS-DOS. PROLOG-based expert system development environment. Integrates tightly with Arity's PROLOG system and SQL interface. Interfaces with existing C, Pascal, FORTRAN, and assembly language applications.

Artelligence, Inc.
14902 Preston Road, Suite 212-252
Dallas, Texas 75240
(214) 437-0361
OPS5 +, $3,000; Prodigy, $450/950

Auto-Intelligence: $490; Intelligence Compiler: $490
IntelligenceWare Inc.
9800 South Sepulveda Boulevard Suite 730
Los Angeles, California 90045
(213) 417-8896
Auto-intelligence generates expert systems for a variety of structured selection and heuristic classification tasks in which experts make decisions among alternatives based on available criteria (diagnosis, consultation, risk analysis, etc.). Can be embedded in LISP, PROLOG, Guru, and the Intelligence Compiler.

Automata Design Associates
1570 Arran Way
Dresher, Pennsylvania 19025
(215) 355-5400
UNXLISP, $86

California Intelligence
912 Powell Street #8
San Francisco, California 94108
(415) 391-4846
XSYS, $995

CLIPS: $250 ($62 for documentation)
COSMIC
University of Georgia
382 East Broad Street
Athens, Georgia 30602
(404) 542-3265
Machine independent; runs under any C compiler. Expert system shell originally developed by the National Aeronautics and Space Administration; now being used for commercial applications.

CRIL
12 Bis, Rue Jean-Jaures
92807 Puteaux, France
1-776-34-37
Le LISP, $3,000

Cybermetrics
P.O. Box 1194
Los Gatos, California 95031
(408) 725-1344
UNXLISP, $69.95

CxPERT: $795 for object code version; $2,000-$4,000 for source license available
Software Plus
1652 Albemarle Drive
Crofton, Maryland 21114
(301) 261-0264
Object code version is available for the IBM PC and compatibles. Source code version is written in C and can be compiled on any machine. Object code version runs under MS-DOS.

Digital Equipment Corp.
146 Main Street
Maynard, Massachusetts 61754
806-Digital
GCLISP, $495; ISI-Interlisp, $10,000

Dynamic Master Systems, Inc.
P.O. Box 566456
Atlanta, Georgia 30356
(404) 565-0771
TOPSI, $175

Easy Expert: $49.95
Park Row
4640 Jewel Street, Suite 232
San Diego, California 92109
(619) 581-6778
Available for the IBM PC and compatibles. Runs under the MS-DOS. Low-cost, user friendly-system for developers and users.

ESIE: $145
Lightwave
P.O. Box 16858
Tampa, Florida 33617
(813) 988-5033
Available for the IBM PC and compatibles. Runs under MS-DOS.

ESP Advisor: $895; ESP Frame Engine: $895; Advisor-2: $895
Expert Systems International
1700 Walnut Street
Philadelphia, Pennsylvania 19103
(215) 735-8510
Available for the IBM PC, DEC VAX, MicroVAX, Sun, and Apollo workstations.
Run under MS-DOS, VMS, and UNIX. ESP Advisor is a rule-based system. ESP
Frame Engine is a frame-based system that supports forward- and backward-chaining
rules. Advisor-2 is an enhanced rule-based system that provides direct access to Lotus
1-2-3, dBASE, GEM graphics, C, FORTRAN, Pascal, and PROLOG.

Expert Controller: $10,000
Umecorp (formerly Ultimate Media Corp.)
45 San Clemente Drive
Corte Madera, California 94939
(415) 924-6700
Development is done on the IBM PC/AT and compatibles, and then ported to
proprietary hardware. Runs under KEOS. Expert system primarily for engineering
and manufacturing control.

Expert-Ease: $695; Expert Edge: $1,495
Jeffrey Perrone and Associates Inc.
3685 Seventeenth Street
San Francisco, California 94114
(415) 431-9562
Expert-Ease is available for the IBM PC/XT and some compatibles. Expert Edge runs
on the IBM PC/XT, PS/2, and compatibles. Both run under MS-DOS. Expert Ease is
an induction-based expert system development tool. Expert Edge features Bayesian
statistics to handle uncertainty.

Expert Systems, Inc.
868 West End Avenue, Suite 3A
New York, New York 10025
(212) 662-7206
Expert Ease, $475

ExperTelligence, Inc.
559 San Ysidro Road
Santa Barbara, California 93108
(805) 969-7874
ExperOPs5, $325

ExperTelligence
559 San Ysidro Road
Santa Barbara, California 93108
(805) 969-3345
ExperLISP, $325

Expert-2: $70; MMSFORTH: $1,180 for site license, $180 for one person on one
computer
Miller Microcomputer Services
61 Lake Shore Road
Natick, Massachusetts 017600-2099
(508) 653-6136
Expert-2 is available for the IBM PC and compatibles, PS/2, and Radio Shack TRS 80.
Runs under MS-DOS. It is an expert system shell for development in MMS Forth,
which has special built-in facilities for prototyping such systems.

EXSYS: $395 and up, depending on Central Processing Unit
EXSYS Inc.
P.O. Box 11247
Albuquerque, New Mexico 87192-0247
(505) 256-8356

Available for the VAX, IBM PC/XT and compatible, PS/2, and some UNIX machines.
Runs under VMS, UNIX, and MS-DOS. Allows experts in a field to configure easily
an expert system that uses their knowledge. Previous programming experience not
necessary.

Franz, Inc.
1141 Harbor Bay Parkway
Alameda, California 94501
(415) 769-5656
FranzLISP

1st CLASS Fusion: $1,495; 1st CLASS HT: $2,495
1st-CLASS Expert Systems Inc.
526 Boston Post Road
Wayland, Massachusetts 01788
(508) 358-7722

Available for the IBM PC. Runs under MS-DOS. A combination of a chaining expert system shell, code generators, graphics capture and display utilities, and database interface.

General Research Corp.
7655 Old Springhouse Road
McLean, Virginia 22102
(703) 893-5915
TIMM, $9,500

GOLDWORKS II: $7,500
Gold Hill Computers Inc.
26 Landsdowne Street
Cambridge, Massachusetts 02139
(617) 621-3300
Available for the IBM/AT, PS/2, and Compaq 386. Runs under MS-DOS and OS/2. Industrial-strength shell for the PC that includes a menu interface to aid novice AI developers.

Gnosis, Inc.
4005 Chesnut Street
Philadelphia, Pennsylvania 19104
(215) 387-1500
P-LISP, $79.95; Apple

Guru: $6,500 for single-user system; $9,900 for LAN version
MDBS Inc.
P.O. Box 248
Lafayette, Indiana 47902
(317) 463-2581
Available for the IBM PC and compatibles, RT-PC, PS/2, VAX, and Sun workstations. Run under MS-DOS, OS/2, Sun, UNIX, and VMS. Expert environment for business application development with easy access to database, spreadsheet, and word processing programs.

Human Edge Software Corp.
2445 Faber Place
Palo Alto, California 94303
(800) 624-5227
Expert Edge, $795; Expert Ease, $475

HUMBLE: $395 (Macintosh and Personal Computers)
Xerox Special Information Systems
250 North Halstead Street
Pasadena, California 91107
(818) 351-2351

Available for many Xerox machines, Macintosh, Sun workstations, and some Tektronix machines.   Runs in Smalltalk/80 environment.   Shell for development in the Smalltalk/80 environment.

Inference Corp.
5300 West Century Boulevard
Los Angeles, California 90045
ART

Information Builders
1250 Broadway
New York, New York 10004
(212) 736-4433
Level 5, $685

Instant Expert 2.0: $69.95; Instant Expert Plus: $498; NEXUS: $698
Human Intellect Systems
1670 South Amphlett Boulevard, #326
San Mateo, California 94402
(415) 571-5939
Instant Expert and Instant Expert Plus are available for the Atari ST, IBM PC/XT, and Macintosh. NEXUS is available for the IBM PC/XT. All three run under GEM. Instant Expert and Instant Expert Plus also run under MS-DOS and Macintosh operating systems.   These products take a classic approach to expert systems development that relies on forward and backward chaining and mixed logic. NEXUS is a combination shell and procedural language.

Integral Quality, Inc.
P.O. Box 31970
Seattle, Washington 31970
(206) 527-2918
IQLISP, $175

IQ-200: $495
Baldur Systems Corp.
3423 Investment Boulevard, Suite 12
Hayward, California 94545
(415) 732-9715

Available for the IBM PC/XT/AT. Runs under MS-DOS. Provides intelligent PC and mainframe distributing computational capability and access to mainframe databases.

IOTC
P.O. Box 1365
Laramie, Wyoming 82070
(307) 721-5818
PC-LISP, $125

KDS3+: $1,495
KDS Corp.
934 Hunter Road.
Wilmette, Illinois 60091
(312) 251-2621
Available for the IBM PC/XT/AT and Apollo workstation under MS-DOS compatibility mode. Runs under MS-DOS. A large-capacity system, KDS3+ produces rules from facts, uses if-then statements, and Explorer and Xerox LISP machines. Does simultaneous inductive and deductive processing.

KEE: (Knowledge Engineering Environment) System
$15,000-$98,000
IntelliCorp Inc.
1975 El Camino Real West
Mountain View, California 94040
(800) KEE-0123
Available on VAX, Sun, Apollo, Symbolics, micro-Explorer, and Explorer workstations: IBM RT PC:
Compaq 386 machines.
Runs under a variety of operating systems. Classic expert system shell suited for development in large corporate environments.

Kemp-Carraway Heart Institute
1600 North Twenty-sixth
Birmingham, Alabama 35234
(205) 226-6697
FLOPS, $495

KES: $4,000 for IBM compatibles; $7,000 for Sun and Apollo machines.
Software Architecture and Engineering Incorporated
1600 Wilson Boulevard, #500
Arlington, Virginia 22209
(703) 276-7910
Available for the Unisys product line, Prime computers, Sun and Apollo workstations, HP UNIX machines, Gould computers, AT&T's 3B2, Silicon Graphics workstations, the IBM PC and compatibles, and IBM RT PC. Runs under XENIX, UNIX, MVS, and

MS-DOS. Full object-oriented expert system shell, designed to be linked to C-mode modules.

Keystone: $9,750 for developer's package; $4,000 for single-user system
Keystone Technologies
7400 Bay Meadows Way Suite 320
Jacksonville, Florida 32216
(904) 737-9634

Levien Instrument
Box 31
McDowell, Virginia 24458
(703) 396-3345
BYSO LISP, $150

LISP Company
430 Monterey Avenue, #4
Los Gatos, California 95030
(408) 354-3668
TLC-LISP 86, $169

Microsoft, Corp.
10700 Northup Way
P.O. Box 97200
Bellevue, Washington 98009
(206) 454-2030
muLISP, $300

Mountain View Press, Inc.
P.O. Box 4656
Mountain View, California 94040
(415) 961-4103
Expert-2, $100

MVP-FORTH Expert-2: $175
Mountain View Press Inc.
P.O. Drawer X
Mountain View, California 94040
(415) 961-4103
Available for the IBM PC/XT/AT and compatibles and Apple II. Runs under MS-DOS and Apple II operating system. Supports object-oriented expert system development.

Neuron Data Inc.
444 High Street
Palo Alto, California 94301
(415) 321-4488
Nexpert, $5,000

Norell Data Systems
P.O. Box 70127
3400 Wilshire Boulevard
Los Angeles, California 90010
(213) 748-5978
LISP/88, $49.95

Northwest Computer Algorithms
P.O. Box 90995
Bellevue, Washington 98009
(800) 426-9400
UO-LISP, $150

PC/BLUE Users Group
New York Amateur Computer Club Inc.
Box 106, Church Street Station
New York, New York 10008
XLISP, $7

Pro Code International
15930 Southwest Colony Place
Portland, Oregon 97224
(800) LIP-4000
Waltz LISP, $169

Production Systems Technologies, Inc.
642 Gettysburg Street
Pittsburgh, Pennsylvania 15206
(412) 362-3117
OPS/83, $1,950-$25,000

Radian Corp.
8501 Mo-Pac Boulevard
P.O. Box 9948
Austin, Texas
(512) 454-4797
Rule Master, $5,000

RK Software
(215) 436-4570
Small-X, $225

Software Intelligence Laboratory, Inc.
1593 Locust Avenue
Bohemia, New York 11716
(516) 589-1676
WIZDOM, $250

Software Toolworks
15223 Ventura Boulevard, Suite 1118
Sherman Oaks, California 91403
LISP/80, $39.95

Solution Systems
541 Main Street Suite 410
South Weymouth, Massachusetts 02190
(617) 337-6963
TransLISP, $95

System Designers Software
5203 Leesburg Pike
Falls Church, Virginia 22041
(703) 820-2700
(LISP + Prolog); POPLOG, $1,950

SRI International
333 Ravenswood Avenue
Menlo Park, California 94301
(415) 859-2464
Series, $5,000

Teknowledge, Inc.
525 University Avenue, Suite 200
Palo Alto, California 94301
(415) 327-6640
M.1, $5,000

Texas Instruments, Inc.
P.O. Box 809063
Dallas, Texas 75380
(800) 527-3500
Personal Consultant Plus, $2950

Ultimate Media, Inc.
275 Magnolia Avenue
Larkspur, California 94939
(415) 924-3644
Advisor, $100

University of Utah
Computer Science Department
3190 MEB
Salt Lake City, Utah 84112
(801) 581-8224
Portable Standard LISP, $750

Xerox
250 North Halstead Street
P.O. Box 7018
Pasadena, California 91109
(818) 351-2351
Humble (Smalltalk)

AI PUBLICATIONS

AI Expert
2443 Filmore Street
Suite 500
San Francisco, California 94115

AI Magazine (quarterly)
American Association for Artificial Intelligence
445 Burgess Drive
Menlo Park, California 94025

AI Trends Newsletter
DM Data, Inc.
6900 East Camelback Road
Scottsdale, Arizona 85251

Applied Artificial Intelligence Reporter (monthly)
ICS - University of Miami
P.O. Box 248235
Coral Gables, Florida 33124

Artificial Intelligence Markets
AIM Publications, Inc.
P.O. Box 156
Natick, Massachusetts 01760

Artificial Intelligence Report
SRI International
3600 West Bayshore Road
Palo Alto, California 94303

Artificial Intelligence Report
Booz-Allen & Hamilton
4330 East-West Highway
Bethesda, Maryland 20814

Expert Systems Journal
Learned Information
Besselsleigh Road
Abingdon, Oxford
OX136LG United Kingdom

Expert System Strategies
Cutter Information
1100 Massachusetts Avenue
Arlington, Massachusetts 02174-9990

Expert System User Magazine
Cromwell House
20 Bride Lane
London EC48DX United Kingdom

IEEE Expert (quarterly)
345 East Forty-seventh Street
New York, New York 10017

Intelligence
P.O. Box 20008
New York, New York 10025

International Journal of Intelligent Systems
John Wiley and Sons
605 Third Avenue
New York, New York 10158

Journal of Automated Reasoning
Kluwer Academic Publishers
101 Phillip Drive
Norwell, Massachusetts 02061

Knowledge Engineering
Richmond Research
Box 366, Village Station
201 Varick Street
New York, New York 10014

Release 1.0
Ziff-Davis Publishing Co.
One Park Avenue
New York, New York 10016

APPENDIX C:
SELECTED BIBLIOGRAPHY ON POLICING

BOOKS

Archambeault, W. G., and B. J. Archambeault. 1984. *Computers
    in criminal justice administration and management: Introduction
    to emerging issues and applications.* Cincinnati: Andersen.
With an emphasis on microcomputer applications to
criminal justice organizations, this book explores the
implications of an automated, dependent society.

Bopp, W. J., and P. Whisenand. 1980. *Police personnel
    administration.* Boston: Allyn and Bacon.
General issues surrounding the police role and organization
of the department are avoided in this text. The bulk of this
work is devoted to recruitment, selection, performance
appraisal, promotion and assignment, job design and
analysis, and affirmative action.

Coleman, P. V. 1987. *What is the future of retired peace officer as
    volunteers in law enforcement?* An independent study
    presented to POST Command College. Sacramento, CA:
    California Commission on Peace Officer Standards and
    Training.
Identifies five trends that police administrators should be
aware of for the future: the growth of technology and its
implications for law enforcement; demographic trends,
particularly those involving increasing numbers of people
grouped by age; diminishing resources and rising costs for

police operations and alternative resource options; increasing performance and efficiency in law enforcement; and law-related trends that affect policing.

Colton. K. W. 1978. *Police computer technology.* Lexington, Mass.: D.C. Heath.
A book that, although somewhat dated, provides a good overview of the use of computers by police, along with a description of various usages of computer-assisted police resource allocation methods. Also identifies a variety of technological innovations in the command and control field and examines the prospects of technology for the future.

Colton, K. W., M. L. Brandeau, and J. M. Tien. 1983. *A national assessment of police command, control, and communications systems.* Washington, D.C.: National Institute of Justice.
Provides a national assessment of police command, control, and communication (PCCC) systems. Computer aided dispatch, mobile digital communications, automated vehicle monitoring, and 911 communications are the focuses of attention. The report stresses the need for specific evaluation of PCCC systems and maintains that a PCCC information clearinghouse to facilitate the transfer of ideas and technologies would be helpful.

Eck, J. E. 1979. *Managing case assignments: The burglary investigation decision model.* Washington, D.C.: Police Executive Research Forum.
An empirical replication study conducted in the Police Executive Research Forum's twenty-six member departments that is based on a model for screening burglary cases prior to assignment. Results suggest that police managers should use screening instruments in the assignment of burglary cases.

Eisenberg, T. 1973. *Police personnel practices in state and local governments.* Washington, D.C.: Police Foundation.
A questionnaire was distributed to 493 police agencies identifying personnel practices. Results suggest that personnel practices differ primarily because of regional variation.

Farmer, D. J. 1984. *Crime control: The use and misuse of police resources.* New York: Plenum.

A socioeconomic text that provides police administrators with a practical resource allocation approach to managing a police department. Describes resource allocation practices in use and cites the major research studies that identify a need to revamp police field operations.

Fyfe, J. J. 1985. *Police management today—issues and case studies.* Washington, D.C.: International City Management Association.
Contains articles that target contemporary issues confronting police administrators, ranging from leadership and management to quality circles in police departments.

Geller, W. A. 1985. *Police leadership in America: Crisis and opportunity.* Chicago: American Bar Association.
Presents two themes: The first issue deals with who runs the police and who should. The second issue addresses the fact that the police continue to operate in a state of crisis. Change is possible because of a new breed of strong police leaders.

Gottfredson, M. R. 1988. *Decision making in criminal justice: Toward the rational exercise of discretion.* New York: Plenum.
An insightful analysis of discretionary decision-making and factors affecting it at various stages in the criminal justice process using a rationalistic and practical frame of reference. The author maintains that facts and the application of scientific methodology to the decision-making processes of the criminal justice system offer the best hope for improving the system.

Hanna, D. G. 1987. *Police chiefs handbook on developmental and power management.* Springfield: Thomas.
An insightful handbook written by a practitioner that addresses police leadership in a development and power management context, with an emphasis on survival techniques necessary to grapple with the harsh realities of bureaucratized management in the public sector.

Hernandez, E. 1982. *Police handbook for applying the systems approach and computer technology.* El Toro, Calif.: Frontline.

A handbook outlining how the police manager can take better advantage of current computer technology utilizing a systems approach. The chapter on the eight functional uses of management information systems is a good one for actual and would-be police administrators.

Hewitt, W. H. 1975. *New directions in police personnel administration: Lateral entry and transferability of retirement credits.*
Lexington, Mass.: Lexington.
Presents both sides of the argument on whether to allow police personnel to move into different areas of the department without losing rank or pension funds.

Holden, R. N. 1986. *Modern police management.* Englewood Cliffs, N.J.: Prentice-Hall.
Addresses police administrative issues and critiques existing police organizational structure. The book advocates a participatory style of management, decentralization, and delegation. Case studies are included in each chapter, along with a summary of court cases involving civil suits against police administrators.

Homant, R. J., and D. B. Kennedy. 1985. *Police and law enforcement, 1975-1981* - volume 3. New York: AMS.
Focuses on eight subject areas: orientation to the police role, police-community relations, the impact of policing on police officers, police discretion and the use of deadly force, hostages and terrorist acts, new police responses to contemporary problems, private police, and professionalization. Contains forty-seven articles written between 1975 and 1981.

Kee, J., and R. C. Larson. 1985. *The potential impact of expert systems in urban police services.* Cambridge, Mass.: MIT.
Expert systems hold great potential for urban police services. Two applications--the ordering of incoming 911 emergency calls and the dispatch of police units to service these calls--are detailed.

Klockars, C. B. 1985. *Idea of police.* Newbury Park, Calif.: Sage.
Addresses justifications for a professional police force, police responsibilities and the role of discretion and external controls in the discharge of duties, and the characteristics of good policing.

Lee, I-J., and R. C. Larson. 1984. *Computer-aided dispatch system as a decision making tool in public and private sectors.* Cambridge, Mass.: MIT.
Surveys areas where a real-time computer-aided dispatch (CAD) system has been applied to the allocation of scarce resources. Through the growth of computer technology, CAD systems can assist dispatchers by increasing productivity and improving response time.

Lynch, R. G. 1986. *Police manager--professional leadership skills.* New York: Random.
Good summary of existing management issues affecting law enforcement agencies: the use of power, civil liability, labor relations, promotions, and the effect of change and conflict on police organizations.

More, H. W. 1985. *Critical issues in law enforcement.* Cincinnati: Andersen.
A well-written and thorough text that confronts perennial problems in policing, among them the police role in a democratic society, the use of deadly force, police professionalization, unionization, discretion, terrorism, organized crime, and stress.

More, H. W., and J. P. Kenney. 1986. *The police executive handbook.* Springfield, Ill.: Thomas.
Presents the results of a survey of chiefs of police in medium to small police departments to discover what they believe are the most significant problems facing them. The authors address such police management issues as work schedules, budgets, communications, and evaluation. A vast array of critical topics such as labor relations, political relationships, and deadly force are explored in detail.

Palmiotti, M. J. 1988. *Critical issues in criminal investigation.* Cincinnati: Andersen.
Interesting exploration of more important issues confronting criminal investigation. The articles range from such subjects as ethics and training to crime-pattern analysis and computer-related crimes.

Pinkele, C. F., and W. C. Louthan. 1985. Politics of police
     discretion. In *Discretion, justice, and democracy: A public
     policy perspective*, ed. C. F. Pinkele and W. C. Louthan.
     Ames, IA: Iowa State.
An examination of many obstacles limiting efforts to
control police discretion. Police discretion is a low-priority
issue with municipal governments, political and legal
roadblocks prevent formal rules from being created to
control police discretion, and the development of law
enforcement rules to create uniformity in decision-making
may be in violation of state laws.

Robinette, H. M. 1987. *Burnout in blue: Managing the police marginal
     performer.* Westport, Conn.: Greenwood.
A practical book that guides police supervisors in
identifying and taking corrective measures to handle
marginal performers. Part of the text is based on results
from a national survey of police supervisory personnel that
focused on their perceptions of poor employee performance.

Rozenberg, J. 1987. *The case for the crown.* Wellingborough,
     Great Britain: Equation.
An excellent description of the background and events
leading to Britian's first independent prosecution service.
Particulary informative on the relations between police and
prosecutor. Required reading for those who are interested
in viewing law enforcement and prosecution from another
perspective.

Shearing, C. D., and P. C. Stenning. 1987. *Private policing.*
     Newbury Park, Calif.: Sage.
A series of essays that police at all levels will find
interesting. Private policing has been largely ignored by
academicians and practitioners until recently. This
collection of papers questions traditional distinctions of
public and private order and, but more important, adds to
our understanding of the police role in the context of
modern democratic governments.

Skolnick, J. H. 1975. *Justice without trial: Law enforcement in a
     democratic society.* New York: Wiley.
A frequently cited book that addresses issues surrounding
urban police organizations, culture, and discretionary

decision-making. An epilogue on the politics of policing is included.

Skolnick, J. H., and D. H. Bayley. 1986. *The new blue line: Police innovation in six American cities.* New York: Free.
A valuable book that demonstrates the application of creative ideas in the police departments of six American cities. These new approaches include strong police-community relations, command decentralization, increased foot patrols, and the expanding role of civilian employees in certain police operations.

Southgate, P. 1988. *New directions in police training.* London: Her Majesty's Stationary Office.
Addresses current training needs of the police and the conversion of them into practical training approaches. The major theme is that training should focus on the development of social skills because of a police officer's frequent contacts with the public. An ancillary concern addressed is that training should foster an atmosphere where positive views and attitudes develop.

Trautman, N. E. 1987. *Law enforcement in-service training programs: Practical and realistic solutions to law enforcement's in-service training dilemma.* Springfield, Ill.: Thomas.
A guidebook for police training administrators that explains how to create and implement training programs. Topics include training strategies, goals, reasons for failure, equipment, budgeting, and managerial support.

U.S. Congress. Office of Technology Assessment. 1986. *Electronic record systems and individual privacy.* Washington, D.C.: Federal Government Information Technology.
Discusses technological developments pertinent to public record keeping, current and future use of electronic record systems in the federal government, the interaction of technology and privacy issues, and policy and practices that may require congressional action.

U.S. Congress. Office of Technology Assessment. 1988. *Criminal justice: New technologies and the Constitution.* Washington, D.C.: U.S. Government Printing Office.

Provides brief descriptions of the newest criminal justice technologies and addresses the delicate balance between the power of the state and the rights of the individual.

Waldron, J., B. Archambeault, W. Archambeault, L. Carsone, J. Conser, and C. Sutton. 1987. *Microcomputers in criminal justice: Current issues and applications.* Cincinnati: Andersen.
Based on a series of unpublished articles presented to the Academy of Criminal Justice Sciences in 1984, this book is intended to assist criminal justice managers interested in microcomputer use.

Whitaker, G. P., S. Mastrofski, E. Ostrom, R. Parks, and S. Percy. 1982. *Basic issues in police performance.* Washington, D.C.: National Institute of Justice.
A thorough and well-documented report that reviews performance measurement in policing. Difficulties in evaluating police performance are discussed, along with suggestions for improving it. The research represents one of four studies supported by the National Institute of Justice's Performance Measurement Program.

Wilson, T. F., and P. L. Woodard. 1986. *Automated fingerprint identification systems: Technology and policy issues.* Washington, D.C.: Bureau of Justice Statistics.
Automated fingerprint identification systems have had a profound impact on policing. AFIS allows police departments to compare latent prints with thousands or millions of other prints in a short time period. This new technology has improved policing through the detection of alias usage.

ARTICLES

Ammann, E. P., and J. Hey. 1986. Establishing agency personnel
    levels. *Law Enforcement Bulletin.* 55: 16-20.
    Identifies traditional approaches to determine staffing levels
    in police agencies such as community population and
    citizen-police officer per capita as inadequate. The more
    accurate indicators for personnel staffing are based on calls
    for service, investigative caseload, and agency policy and
    procedure.

Bayse, W. A., and C. G. Morris. 1987. FBI automation strategy:
    Developing AI applications for national investigative
    programs. *Signal Magazine.* 41: 185-203.
    Examines the FBI's efforts to take advantage of the most
    sophisticated crime technology available. Since 1977, the
    FBI has applied artificial intelligence to its various
    investigative branches with success.

Birchler, M. R. 1988. The future of law enforcement: Laptop
    computers. *Police Chief.* 55: 28-30.
    Explores the benefits and deficiencies of using laptop
    computers in police departments. The author asserts that as
    police departments move toward microcomputer use, more
    attention will be given to laptop computers.

Cameron, J. 1988. Artificial intelligence: Expert systems,
    microcomputers and law enforcement. *Law and Order.*
    36: 58-66.
    Discusses the potential utility of expert systems for police
    administrators and highlights some current applications of
    this technology.

Chappell, D., R. Gordon, and R. Moore. 1983. Selection, training
    and evaluation of crime investigators - a Canadian
    survey. *Canadian Police College Journal.* 7: 271-296.
    Reports on a survey of municipal police departments in
    Canada that found that 60 percent of the forces give some
    preparatory training, with the bulk of the forces providing
    for their investigators to attend a regional training center.
    Results also demonstrate that most forces rely on factors
    such as arrest rates, clearance rates, and conviction rates to

evaluate performance, but there is an emerging need to find alternatives to these traditional and unreliable criteria.

Clark, C. W., and D. Maus. 1988. Selection and installation of a mobile digital communications system. *Police Chief.* 55: 36-40.
Highlights the advantages of the Long Beach, California, Police Department's mobile digital communications system adaptable for police vehicles. One of the most often cited advantages is the ability of the system to transmit sensitive information digitally, bypassing the criminal element and the public at large who operate scanners.

Clede, B. 1986. Micro-computers on patrol. *Law and Order.* 36: 36-42.
Examines the impact of computer innovation on policing operations. Mobile data terminals, computer-aided dispatch software, vehicle tracking systems and computer-issued tickets are featured.

Coady, W. F. 1987. Investigating with APES (Augmented Prolog Expert System). *Security Management.* 31: 67-70.
Examines Augmented Prolog Expert System (APES), a system that permits the investigator to enter data, receive the computer's answer, and then respond to the solution provided by the computer. The system distributes expert information to the user to assist in solving a crime.

Doering, R. D., and D. E. Clapp. 1976. Management study of command/control operations at Orlando police department. *Journal of Police Science and Administration.* 4: 94-105.
Describes a command/control system in the Orlando Police Department.

Fitzpatrick, M. J. 1988. Selecting an automated fingerprint identification system. *Law Enforcement Bulletin.* 57: 7-11.
Suggests that a comprehensive benchmark test with detailed documentation and evaluation will provide administrators with objective criteria to select an automated fingerprint identification system to replace labor-intensive manual fingerprint systems.

Frost, T. M., and M. J. Seng. 1984. Police entry level curriculum:
    A thirty year perspective. *Journal of Police Science and
    Administration.* 12: 251-259.
    Shows, using the Frost study as a benchmark of change, that
    police entry-level training has been remarkably consistent,
    with little modification in the past thirty years.

Fyfe, J. J. 1986. Police personnel practices, 1986. *Baseline Data
    Report.* 18: 1-11.
    Municipal policing has undergone many changes since 1982
    when budgetary constraints and the effects of inflation were
    major concerns of top policymakers in police departments.
    Data from 1986 suggest that while dollar shortages continue
    to affect most law enforcement agencies negatively, the
    effects of scarce dollars are not a pervasive as they were
    four years ago.

Griffen, G. R., R. L. Dunbar, and M. E. McGill. 1978. Factors
    associated with job satisfaction among police personnel.
    Journal of Police Science and Administration. 6: 77-85.
    Examines education and job satisfaction and factors
    associated with job satisfaction.

Handberg, R., H. F. Hill, and R. F. Daroszewski. 1985. Measuring
    police performance for political accountability: The law
    enforcement service standard. *Journal of Police Science
    and Administration.* 13: 53-57.
    Describes the Orange County, Florida, police department's
    model that links available fiscal resources to levels of
    service in a police agency. The Law Enforcement Service
    Standard used takes shifting political and municipal fiscal
    priorities into account in the allocation of resources to the
    local law enforcement agency.

Hayes, C. 1987. The impact of recent research on the detective
    role. *Police Journal.* 60: 97-109.
    The efficiency of detective units moved to the forefront of
    research in the 1980's, while inquiries on how investigators
    clear cases diminished.

Haygood, S. B. 1988. Cops and computers: How compatible? *Law
    Enforcement Technology.* 15: 26-30.
    Surveys five general areas in which computer technology
    can be applied to law enforcement functions: text

processing, archival, analysis, simulation, and artificial intelligence.

Hernandez, A. P. 1986. Is law enforcement ready for the
    artificial intelligence explosion? *Police Chief.* 53: 50-52.
Describes the current popularity of artificial intelligence systems in the commercial world. The author suggests that the law enforcement community should capitalize on this innovative technology and then describes areas where AI applications could prove useful in solving problems that plague police departments.

Icove, D. J. 1986. Automated crime profiling. *Law Enforcement
    Bulletin.* 55: 1-4.
Highlights the FBI's National Center for the Analysis of Violent Crime and demonstrates how this section has been taking advantage of the power of artificial intelligence through the automation of the criminal personality.

Kelly, K. F., J. J. Rankin, and R. C. Wink. 1987. Method and
    applications of DNA fingerprinting: A guide for the non-
    scientist. *Criminal Law Review.* February: 105-110.
Discusses DNA fingerprinting and its implications for the criminal and civil justice system.

Kemp, R. L., and H. A. Fischer. 1987. More on police
    productivity: Beyond cutback to creativity. *Journal of
    Forensic Science Society.* 27: 89-92.
Examines how limited financial resources have caused police management practices to turn creativity, innovation, and productivity. The author maintains that improved management practices in the delivery of services is important in restoring confidence in government.

Kleiman, L. S., and M. E. Gordon. 1986. An examination of the
    relationship between police training academy
    performance and job performance. *Journal of Police
    Science and Administration.* 14: 293-299.
Shows that training performance may not be a strong correlate with on-the-job performance because of the moderating effects of intelligence and conformity.

Law and Order. 1988. Digital technology streamlines criminal
    justice information system. *Law and Order.* 36: 107-110.
    Looks at the Dayton Police Department, one of the most
    progressive law enforcement agencies in the nation, in terms
    of computerizing service functions. This department utilizes
    digital technology that records officers' spoken words on
    hard disks.

Law Enforcement News. 1987. Detectives' know-how grafted
    onto computer. *Law Enforcement News,* July: 1.
    An examination of the Baltimore County Police
    Department's intelligent system to simulate the thought
    processes of residential burglary detectives.

Leonard-Barton, D., and J. J. Sviokla. 1988. Putting expert
    systems to work. *Harvard Business Review.* 88: 91-98.
    Reports on the real benefits of expert systems in the design,
    diagnosis, and monitoring in a range of industries, from
    computers to accounting. Details the success of such expert
    systems as N L Baroid Company's MUDMAN and Digital
    Equipment Corporation's XCON.

Levine, C. H. 1986. Police management in the 1980s: From
    decrementalism to strategic thinking. *Public Administration
    Review.* 45: 691-700.
    Addresses the need of police administrators to grapple with
    the problems of fiscal stress to maintain organizational
    effectiveness and advocates a strategic management
    approach. Such strategic responses require a multiyear time
    frame (usually three to five years); a significant reallocation
    and reconfiguration of resources; substantial changes in the
    organizational structure and work force; and a
    comprehensive as opposed to an ad hoc reexamination of
    the organization's problems, mission, and structure.

Linden, E. 1988. Putting knowledge to work. *Time,* March 28:
    60-63.
    Describes how artificial intelligence is revolutionizing the
    way business and government make decisions.

McCabe, J. P. 1988. Big city chief tells what it takes. *Law
    Enforcement Technology.* 15: 10-14.
    Addresses some of the most pressing concerns that police
    chiefs will face: personnel distribution, AIDS awareness

training, deadly force, corruption, training of recruits, postacademy training, minority hiring, and women in policing.

McCampbell, M. S. 1987. A national perspective of field training officer programs. *Law and Order.* 35: 23-24.
A survey of 588 state and municipal police departments to secure data about field training officer programs.

McLaughlin, C. V., and R. L. Bing III. 1987. Law enforcement personnel selection: A commentary. *Journal of Police Science and Administration.* 15: 271-276.
Details the role of affirmative action, politics, and the competence of police recruits in the selection and retention of law enforcement personnel. The authors maintain that future police selection practices will depend on political factors, perceived public need, legislation, and courtroom mandates.

Malouff, J. M., and N. S. Schutte. 1986. Using biographic information to hire the best new police officers: Research findings. *Journal of Police Science and Administration.* 14: 175-177.
Turnover, poor productivity, and other personnel problems result when police administrators select inappropriate employees. This article identifies four biographical items that have been shown to predict future performance and urges police agencies to make sure information in these areas is accurate.

Meese, E. 1987. DOJ's role in law enforcement education and training. *Police Chief.* 54: 10.
A look at the Department of Justice's training and education efforts at the state and local law enforcement levels.

Meese, E. 1988. DNA research providing powerful investigative tool. *Police Chief.* 55: 10.
Examines one of the most promising developments in high technology to improve law enforcement officers' crime-solving capabilities: the successful use of DNA testing as a means of identifying suspects. Research efforts are underway to make this technology available to all police crime laboratories.

Metts, J. R. 1985. The police force of tomorrow. *Futurist.*
October: 31-36.
Future police officers will be well trained, educated, and enjoy the professional status that doctors and lawyers now have. As society becomes more complex and demanding, the role of the police officer will change. As such, training standards will be raised. Police administrators will care less about marksmanship and physique and more about mental capacity, human relations skills, and diplomas.

Moran, J., and K. Layne. 1988. Enhanced 9-1-1/CAD: interfacing new technology to fight crime. *Police Chief.* 55: 25-29.
Describes the 9-1-1/computer-assisted dispatch system utilized in the Las Vegas Metropolitan Police Department and discusses problems created by the 9-1-1/CAD interface.

Moses, K. 1987. The promise fulfilled: Making local AFIS systems work. *Police Chief.* 54: 50-57.
Cites the three corollaries involved in the success of automated fingerprint identification systems, discusses planning considerations and shopping for the appropriate AFIS system, and concludes by asserting that fingerprint computers have the potential for being the second most important tool the police have to fight crime.

Pogoloff, K. 1988. Computers animate training. *Law Enforcement Technology.* 15: 52-56.
A report on the San Bernardino County Sheriff's Department's exploration of how improvements in training technology can enhance the performance of officers. This department has a complete instructional package (though not yet operational) that will test the skill of officers in applying the four basic principles of Miranda.

Prietula, M. J., and H. A. Simon. 1989. The experts in your midst. *Harvard Business Review.* 89: 120-124.
The combination of analysis and intuition that form expertise is often undervalued in organizations. Capitalizing on expert performance means understanding how this expertise contributes to the success of the organization and then justly rewarding it.

Probert, J. 1986. Police telecommunications: The influence of computers on law enforcement. *Police Chief.* May: 53-55.

Ponders the need for standards and guidelines for computerized communications and information-processing programs since there has been a proliferation of these systems.

Reboussin, R. 1988. An expert system designed to profile murderers. Paper presented to the Fortieth Annual Meeting of the American Society of Criminology Conference, 9-12 November, Chicago.
Reports on the application of an expert system to profile murderers at the FBI's Center for the Analysis of Violent Crime.

Schrage, M. 1986. Big Floyd's all wired up to aid G-men. *Washington Post,* 20 July: 1.
Looks at the FBI's "Big Floyd," an expert system designed to help agents solve labor racketeering cases, and other expert system applications used by federal agencies.

Smith, N. 1986. Black Hawk County gains by sharing. *The Police Chief.* 53: 34.
Cites the dramatic improvement the Black Hawk County Criminal Justice Information System has made on the law enforcement agencies in Black Hawk County, Iowa. The computer network has three components: arrest records management system, booking management system, and jail management system.

Smith, P. M. 1988. In-service training for law enforcement personnel. *Law Enforcement Bulletin.* 57: 19-22.
Details improvements in in-service training programs for police personnel to alleviate some of the problems affecting contemporary police administrator.

Stone, B. S. 1988. The high-tech beat in St. Pete. *Police Chief.* 55: 23-24.
Reports on the St. Petersburg Police Department, which leads the country in equipping patrol cars with portable computers and technology.

Sykes, G. W. 1986. Automation, management, and the police role: The new reformers? *Journal of Police Science and Administration.* 14: 24-29.
Explores the nature of the police role and concludes that there is an inherent danger in leading the public to believe

that automation will create a dramatic improvement in curbing crime. However, the efficiency that automation produces will enhance the crime control function.

Tafoya, W. L. 1987. Artificial intelligence. In Eleventh Annual
    Law Enforcement Information Systems Symposium,
    Gaithersburg, Maryland, 19-21 August: 1-15.
    Introduces the concept of artificial intelligence and then discusses some applications for expert systems in law enforcement. Telecommunications, administration, and training are three possible areas in the which expert systems could prove beneficial.

Tully, E. J. 1987. The near-term future: Implications for law
    enforcement. *Canadian Police College Journal.* 11: 89-105.
    A 1985 survey of the world's largest law enforcement agencies reveals that financial resource shortages were the most frequently cited short-term problem. Additional anticipated problems include new types of crime associated with high technology and narcotics, drug abuse by officers, urban unrest, and terrorism.

Walker, R., and C. J. Flammang. 1980. Law enforcement training
    entering the 1980s. *Police Chief.* 47: 60-64.
    Examines the use of PLATO, an automated system designed to assist the law enforcement community in meeting their occupational training needs.

Wilkenson, J., and J. Chattin-McNichols. 1985. The effectiveness
    of computer-assisted instruction for police officers.
    Journal of Police Science and Administration. 13: 230-235.
    Focuses on increased knowledge in a particular area of criminal procedure and on officers' attitudes toward computer-aided instruction.

APPENDIX D:
SELECTED TECHNICAL
BIBLIOGRAPHY

BOOKS

Albus, J. S. 1981. *Brains, behavior and robotics.* New York:
Byte/McGraw-Hill.

Aleksander, I. 1983. *Artificial vision for robots.* New York:
Chapman and Hall/Methuen.

Aleksander, I., and P. Burnett. 1987. *Thinking machines: The
search for artificial intelligence.* London: Roxby.

Andriole, S. J. 1985. *Applications in artificial intelligence.*
Princeton: Petrocelli.

Bainbridge, L. 1986. *Asking questions and accessing knowledge:
Future computing systems.* New York: Elsevier.

Banerji, R. B. 1980. *Artificial intelligence: A theoretical
approach.* New York: North Holland.

Barr, A., and E. A. Feigenbaum. 1982. *The handbook of
artificial intelligence, vols. I-II.* Los Altos, Calif:
William Kaufmann.

Beerel, A. C. 1987. *Expert systems: Strategic implications and
applications.* New York: Wiley.

Beverly, W. T. 1985. *Designing and implementing your own expert system.* New York: Byte/McGraw-Hill.

Boden, M. 1977. *Artificial intelligence and natural man.* New York: Basic.

Booch, G. 1987. *Software engineering with ADA.* Menlo Park, Calif.: Benjamin Cummings.

Brown, J. S. 1984. The low road, the middle road, and the high road. In *The AI business,* ed. P. H. Winston and K. A. Prendergast. Cambridge, Mass.: MIT.

Brownston, L., R. Farrell, E. Kant, and N. Martin. 1985. *Programming expert systems in OPS5: An introduction to rule-based Programming.* Reading, Mass.: Addison-Wesley.

Buchanan, B. G., and E. H. Shortliffe. 1984. *Rule-based expert systems.* Reading, Mass.: Addison-Wesley.

Bundy, A. 1978. *Artificial intelligence: An introductory course.* New York: North Holland.

Bundy, A. 1984. *Catalogue of artificial intelligence tools.* New York: Springer-Verlag.

Charniak, E., and D. V. McDermott. 1985. *Introduction to artificial intelligence.* Reading, Mass.: Addison-Wesley.

Chorafas, D. N. 1987. *Applying expert systems in business.* New York: McGraw-Hill.

Cohen, P. R. and E. A. Feigenbaum. 1982. *The handbook of artificial intelligence, vol. III.* Los Altos, Calif.: William Kaufmann.

Dixon, N. 1981. *Preconscious reasoning.* New York: Wiley.

Feigenbaum, E. 1979. Themes and case studies of knowledge engineering. In *Expert systems in the micro-electronic age,* ed. D. Michie. Edinburgh, Scotland: Edinburgh.

Feigenbaum, E. A., and P. McCorduck. 1983. *The Fifth Generation.* Reading, Mass.: Addison-Wesley.

Forman, E. H., and T. l. Saaty. 1986. *Expert choice.* McLean, Va.: Decision Support Software.

Forsyth, R., and C. Naylor. 1985. *The hitch-hiker's guide to artificial intelligence.* New York: Chapman and Hall/Methuen.

Frenzel, L. E. 1986. *Crash course in artificial intelligence and expert systems.* Indianapolis: Howard W. Sams.

Gloess, P. Y. 1981. *Understanding artificial intelligence.* Sherman Oaks, Calif.: Alfred.

Graham, N. 1979. *Artificial intelligence, making machines "think."* Blue Ridge Summit, Pa.: Tab.

Harmon, P., and D. King. 1985. *Expert systems.* New York: Wiley.

Harmon, P., and D. King. 1985. *Expert systems: Artificial intelligence in business.* New York: Wiley.

Harmon, P., R. Maus, and W. Morrissey. 1988. *Expert system tools and applications.* New York: Wiley.

Harris, M. D. 1985. *Introduction to natural language processing.* Reston, Va.: Reston.

Hayes. J. E., and D. Michie. 1983. *Intelligent systems.* New York: Halstead.

Hayes-Roth, F., D. A. Waterman, and D. B. Lenant. 1983. *Building expert systems.* Reading, Mass.: Addison-Wesley.

Jackson, P. 1986. *Introduction to expert systems.* Reading, Mass.: Addison-Wesley.

Jenkins, R. A. 1986. *Supercomputers of today and tomorrow: The parallel processing revolution.* Blue Ridge Summit, Pa.: Tab.

Klahr, P., and D. Waterman. 1986. *Expert systems: Techniques, tools and applications.* Reading, Mass.: Addison-Wesley.

Krutch, J. 1981. *Experiments in artificial intelligence.*   Indianapolis: Howard W. Sams.

Levine, R., D. E. Drang, and B. Edelson. 1986. *A comprehensive guide to AI and expert systems.* New York: McGraw-Hill.

MacLennan, B. J. 1983. *Principles of programming languages: Design, evaluation, and implementation.* New York: Holt, Rinehart and Winston.

Martin, J., and S. Oxman. 1988. *Building expert systems.* Englewood Cliffs, N.J.: Prentice-Hall.

McCarthy, J. 1958. Programs with common sense. In *Semantic information processing*, ed. M. Minsky. Cambridge, Mass.: MIT.

McCorduck, P. 1979. *Machines who think.* San Francisco: W. H. Freeman.

Michalski, R. S., J. G. Carbonell, and T. M. Mitchell. 1983. *Machine learning: An artificial intelligence approach.* Palo Alto, Calif.: Tioga.

Mischkoff, H. C. 1985. *Understanding artificial intelligence.* Indianapolis: TI/Howard W. Sams.

Moates, D. R., and G. M. Schumacher. 1980. *An introduction to cognitive psychology.* Berkeley, Calif.: Wadsworth.

Nagy, T., D. Gault, and M. Nagy. 1985. *Building your first expert system.* Torrance, Calif.: Ashton-Tate.

Naylor, C. 1988. *Build your own expert system.* New York: Halstead.

Negoita, C. V. 1985. *Expert systems and fuzzy systems.*   Menlo Park, Calif.: Benjamin/Cummings.

Nilsson, N. J. 1980. *Principles of artificial intelligence.*   Palo Alto, Calif.: Tioga.

O'Malley, T. J. 1985. *Artificial intelligence projects for the Commodore 64.* Blue Ridge Summit, Pa.: Tab.

O'Shea, T., and M. Eisenstadt. 1984. *Artificial intelligence tools, techniques and applications.* New York: Harper and Row.

Parsaye, K., and M. Chignell. 1988. *Expert systems for experts.* New York: Wiley.

Peat, F.D. 1985. *Artificial intelligence: How machines think.* New York: Baen.

Rauch-Hindin, W. 1988. *A guide to commercial artificial intelligence.* Englewood Cliffs, N.J.: Prentice-Hall.

Rich, E. 1983. *Artificial intelligence.* New York: McGraw-Hill.

Ritchie, D. 1983. *The binary brain: Artificial intelligence in the age of electronics.* Reading, Mass.: Addison-Wesley.

Saaty, T. L., and K. P. Kerns. 1985. *Analytic planning: Organization of systems.* New York: Pergamon.

Schank, R. C., and P. G. Childers. 1984. *The cognitive computer.* Reading, Mass.: Addison-Wesley.

Schildt, H. 1987. *Artificial intelligence using C.* New York: Osborne McGraw-Hill.

Sell, P. S. 1985. *Expert systems: A practical introduction.* New York: Halstead.

Shapiro, A. D. 1987. *Structured induction in expert systems.* Reading, Mass.: Addison-Wesley.

Shirai, Y., and J. Tsujii. 1984. *Artificial intelligence concepts, techniques, and applications.* New York: Wiley.

Simon, H. A. 1981. *The sciences of the artificial.* Cambridge, Mass.: MIT.

Sprague, K., and S. Ruth. 1988. *Developing expert systems using EXSYS.* Santa Cruz, Calif.: Mitchell.

Stevens, L. 1985. *Artificial intelligence: The search for the perfect machine.* Hasbrouck Heights, N.J.: Hayden.

Tanimoto, S. L. 1987. *The elements of artificial intelligence: An introduction using LISP*. Rockville, Md.: Computer Science.

Townsend, C., and D. Foucht. 1986. *Designing and programming personal expert systems*. Blue Ridge Summit, Pa.: Tab.

Turner, R. 1984. *Logics for artificial intelligence*. Chicester, England: Ellis Horwood

Ullman, J. D. 1982. *Principles of database systems*. Rockville, Md.: Computer Science.

Waterman, D. A. 1986. *A guide to expert systems*. Reading, Mass.: Addison-Wesley.

Weiss, S. M., and C. A. Kulikowski. 1984. *A practical guide to designing expert systems*. Totowa, N.J.: Rowman and Allanheld.

Williamson, M. 1986. *Artificial intelligence for microcomputers*. Bowie, Md.: Brady.

Winston, P. H., and R. H. Brown. 1979. *Artificial intelligence: An MIT perspective vols. I, II*. Cambridge, Mass.: MIT.

Winston, P. M. 1984. *Artificial intelligence*. Reading, Mass.: Addison-Wesley.

Winston, P. H. and K. A. Prendergast. 1984. *The AI business: The commercial uses of artificial intelligence*. Cambridge, Mass.: MIT.

Woods, W. 1975. What's in a link? In *Representation and understanding*, ed. D. Bobrow and A. Collins. New York: Academic.

ARTICLES

Bahill, A. T., P. N. Harris and E. Senn. 1988. Lessons learned: building expert systems. *AI Expert.* 3: 36-45.

Bobrow, D. J., and M. J. Stefik. 1986. Perspectives on artificial intelligence programming. *Science.* February: 28.

Bobrow, D., and T. Winograd. 1977. An overview of KRL, a knowledge representation language. *Cognitive Science.* 1: 3-46.

Carande, R. 1988. Checking out AI sources. *AI Expert.* 3: 60-65.

Chandrasekaran, B. 1983. On evaluating AI systems for medical diagnosis. *AI Magazine.* 4: 34-37.

Chapnick, P. 1987. From data base to knowledge base. *AI Expert.* 2: 7-8.

Coffee, P. C., and D. J. Strauss. 1988. Conventional languages and AI. *AI Expert.* 3: 38-45.

Evanson, S. E. 1988. How to talk to an expert. *AI Expert.* 3: 36-41.

Forgy, C. L., and S. J. Shepard. 1987. RETE: a fast match algorithm. *AI Expert.* 2: 34-40.

Gaines, B. R. 1986. An overview of knowledge acquisition and transfer. Proceedings of the AAAI Knowledge Acquisition Workshop, Banff, Canada.

Hoffman, R. R. 1987. The problem of extracting knowledge of experts from the perspective of experimental psychology. *AI Magazine.* 8: 53-57.

Kahn, G., S. Nowlan, and J. McDermott. 1985. MORE: An intelligent knowledge acquisition tool. Proceedings of the International Joint Conference on Artificial Intelligence, Los Angeles.

Kitto, C., and J. Boose. 1986. Knowledge acquisition dialogues. Proceedings of the Second Annual Expert Systems Conference, Washington, D.C.

MacArthur, L. 1985. Artificial intelligence users in a new society. *Automation News.* 3: 14-15.

McCarthy, J. 1960. Recursive functions of symbolic expressions and their computation by machine. *Communications of the ACM.* 7: 184-195.

McCullough, T. 1987. Six steps to selling AI. *AI Expert.* 2: 55-60.

Marcot, B. 1987. Testing your knowledge base. *AI Expert.* 2: 42-47.

Newquist, H. P. 1988. Braining the expert. *AI Expert.* 3: 67-69.

Newquist. H. P. 1988. Struggling to maintain. *AI Expert.* 3: 69-71.

Newquist, H. P. 1988. The new crime stopper's notebook: The expert system. *AI Expert.* 3: 19-21.

Parsaye, K. 1988. Acquiring and verifying knowledge automatically. *AI Expert.* 3: 48-63.

Parsaye, K., and S. Murphree. 1987. Using auto-intelligence for knowledge and expertise transfer between humans. Proceedings of the Third Annual Artificial Intelligence Conference, April, Long Beach, Calif.

Phillips, J. S., and P. Sanders. 1988. First steps in prototyping. *AI Expert.* 3: 64-68.

Politakis, P., and S. M. Weiss. 1984. Using empirical analysis to refine expert system knowledge bases. *Artificial Intelligence.* 22: 23-48.

Prerau, D. S. 1987. Knowledge acquisition in the development of a large expert system. *AI Magazine.* 8: 43-51.

Rauch-Hindin, W. B. 1988. Problems with paradigms. *AI Expert.* 3: 55-60.

Rolandi, W. G. 1986. Knowledge engineering in practice. *AI Expert.* 1: 58-62.

Rolandi, W. G. 1988. A practical approach to knowledge engineering. *AI Expert.* 3: 60-65.

Salzberg, S. 1987. Knowledge representation in the real world. *AI Expert.* 2: 32-38.

Smith, E. J. 1987. Multiple word searches with LFIND. *Computer Language.* 4: 47-53.

Smith, D. I. 1988. Implementing real world expert systems. *AI Expert.* 3: 51-57.

Stefik, M., D. Bobrow, S. Mittal, and L. Conway. 1983. Knowledge programming in loops. *AI Magazine.* 4: 3-13.

Thompson, B., and B. Thompson. 1987. Structure, bottlenecks, and knowledge acquisition. *AI Expert.* 2: 25-28.

Wilson, L. 1987. Rule-based programming in C. *AI Expert.* 2: 15-21.

REFERENCES

Abelson, M. A., and B. D. Baysinger. 1981. Optimal and
    dysfunctional turnover: Toward an organizational
    level model. *Academy of Management Journal.* 19: 331-341.

Archambeault, W. G., and B. J. Archambeault. 1984.
    *Computers in criminal justice administration and management:
    Introduction to emerging issues and applications.* Cincinnati:
    Andersen.

Baker, R., and F. A. Meyer, Jr. 1979. *Evaluating alternative
    law-enforcement policies.* Lexington, Mass.: D. C. Heath.

Birchler, M. R. 1988. The future of law enforcement: Laptop
    computers. *Police Chief.* 55: 28-30.

Bloch, P. B., and J. Bell. 1976. *Managing investigations: The
    Rochester system.* Washington, D.C.: Police Foundation.

Boland, B., W. Logan, R. Sones, and W. Martin. 1988. *The
    prosecution of felony arrests, 1982.* Washington, D.C.:
    Bureau of Justice Statistics.

Boydston, J. E., and M. E. Sherry. 1975. *San Diego community
    profile: Final report.* Washington, D.C.: Police Foundation.

Boydston, J. E., M. E. Sherry, and N. P. Moelter. 1977. *Patrol
    staffing in San Diego.* Washington, D.C.: Police
    Foundation.

Brand, D., and J. M. Koroloff. 1976. Team policing: Management of criminal investigation. *Police Chief.* 43: 65-67.

Brosi, K. 1979. *A cross-city comparison of felony case processing.* Washington, D.C.: U.S. Government Printing Office.

Cameron, J. 1988. Artificial intelligence: Expert systems, microcomputers and law enforcement. *Law and Order.* 36: 58-66.

Chambers, J. A., and J. W. Sprecher. 1980. Computer-assisted instruction: Current trends and critical issues. *Communications of the ACM.* 23: 332-342.

Chappell, D., R. Gordon, and R. Moore. 1983. Selection, training and evaluation of crime investigators-A Canadian survey. *Canadian Police College Journal.* 7: 271-296.

Church, T. 1978. *Justice delayed: The pace of litigation in urban trial courts.* Williamsburg, Va.: National Center for State Courts.

Clede, B. 1986. Micro-computers on patrol. *Law and Order.* 36: 36-42.

Cole, G. F. 1983. *The American system of criminal justice.* Monterey, Calif.: Brooks/Cole.

Colton, K. W. 1978. *Police computer technology.* Lexington, Mass.: D.C. Heath.

Colton, K. W., M. L. Brandeau, and J. M. Tien. 1983. *A national assessment of police command, control, and communications systems.* Washington, D.C.: National Institute of Justice.

Conklin, J. 1972. *Robbery and the criminal justice system.* Philadelphia: J. B. Lippincott.

Crawford, F., P. Giordano, S. Goldsmith, J. Jacoby, J. Phillips, and A. Sonner. 1989. *Guidebook for the establishment of career criminal programs.* Washington, D.C.: Bureau of Justice Assistance.

Dalton, D. R., and W. D. Tudor. 1979. Turnover turned over: An expanded and positive perspective. *Academy of Management Review.* 4: 225-235.

Doering, R. D., and D. E. Clapp. 1976. Management study of command/control operations at the Orlando police department. *Journal of Police Science and Administration.* 4: 94-105.

Eck, J. E. 1979. *Managing case assignments: The burglary investigation decision model.* Washington, D.C.: Police Executive Research Forum.

Eisenstein, J., and H. Jacob. 1977. *Felony justice: An organizational analysis of criminal courts.* Boston: Little Brown.

Federal Bureau of Investigation. 1987. *Crime in the United States.* Washington, D.C.: U.S. Government Printing Office.

Feeley, M. M. 1983. *Court reform on trial: Why simple solutions fail.* New York: Basic.

Fitzpatrick, M. J. 1988. Selecting an automated fingerprint identification system. *Law Enforcement Bulletin.* 57: 7-11.

Forst, B., J. Lucianovic, and S. Cox. 1978. *What happens after arrest?* Washington, D. C.: Institute for Law and Social Research.

Frenzel, L. E., Jr. 1987. *Crash course in artificial intelligence and expert systems.* Indianapolis: Howard W. Sams.

Fyfe, J. J. 1985. *Police management today-issues and case studies.* Washington, D.C.: International City Management Association.

Garofalo, J., and A. Neuberger. 1987. *Reducing felony case attrition through enhanced police-prosecutor coordination.* Washington, D.C.: National Institute of Justice.

Gilman, H. 1987. Detectives on disks: Law enforcers use new computer software to solve crimes. *Wall Street Journal,* 11 September: 29.

Gladwell, M. 1988. DNA prints: New way to finger criminals. *Washington Post Business Section,* 19 September 6.

Gottfredson, M. R., and D. M. Gottfredson. 1980. *Decision-making in criminal justice: Toward the rational exercise of discretion.* Cambridge: Ballinger.

Government Data Systems. 1973. PATRIC (Pattern recognition and information correlation) system traps suspects by correlating reports. *Government Data Systems.* 1: 18-19.

Greenberg, B., O. Yu, and K. Lang. 1973. *Enhancement of the investigative function vol. 4: Burglary investigative checklist and handbook.* Springfield: National Technical Information Service.

Greenwood, P. W., J. M. Chaiken, J. Petersilia, and L. Prusoff. 1975. *The criminal investigation process, vol. 3: Observations and analysis.* Santa Monica, Calif.: Rand.

Hollenback, J. R., and C. R. Williams. 1986. Turnover functionality versus turnover frequency: A note on work attitudes and organizational effectiveness. *Journal of Applied Psychology.* 71: 606-611.

Icove, D. J. 1986. Automated crime profiling. *FBI Law Enforcement Bulletin.* 55: 1-4.

Jackson, J. S. 1976. Man with machine supports investigator. Paper presented at 1976 Carnahan Conference on Crime Countermeasures, University of Kentucky College of Engineering, Lexington.

Jacoby, J. E. 1980. *The American prosecutor: A search for identity.* Lexington, Mass.: D. C. Heath.

Jacoby, J. E. 1982. *Basic issues in prosecutor and public defender performance.* Washington, D. C.: Bureau of Social Science Research.

Jacoby, J. E., E. C. Ratledge, and R. D. Allen. 1988. *Building an expert system for the Baltimore County Police Department.* Washington D.C.: National Institute of Justice.

Kelling, G. L., T. Pate, D. Dieckman, and C. Brown. 1974. *The Kansas City preventive patrol experiment: A technical report.* Washington, D.C.: Police Foundation.

Kelly, K. F., J. J. Rankin, and R. C. Wink. 1987. Method and applications of DNA fingerprinting: A guide for the non-scientist. *Criminal Law Review.* February: 105-110.

Larson, R. C. 1978. *Police deployment: New tools for planners.* Lexington, Mass.: Lexington.

Law and Order. 1988. Digital technology streamlines criminal justice information system. *Law and Order.* 36: 107-110.

Lee, I-J., and R. C. Larson. 1984. *Computer-aided dispatch system as a decision making tool in public and private sectors.* Cambridge: MIT.

Manili, B., and E. Connors. 1988. *Police chiefs and sheriffs rank their criminal justice needs.* Washington, D.C.: National Institute of Justice.

McDonald, W. F. 1982. *Police-prosecutor relations in the United States: Executive summary.* Washington, D.C.: U.S. Government Printing Office.

McDonald, W. F. 1987. *Improving evidence gathering through a computer-assisted case intake program: Final report.* Washington, D.C.: National Institute of Justice.

McLaughlin, C. V., and R. L. Bing III. 1987. Law enforcement personnel selection: A commentary. *Journal of Police Science and Administration.* 15: 271-276.

Meese, E. 1988. DNA research providing powerful investigative tool. *Police Chief.* 55: 10.

Miller, F. W. 1969. *Prosecution: The decision to charge a suspect with a crime.* Boston: Little, Brown.

Mobley, W. H. 1982. *Employee turnover: Causes, consequences and control.* Reading, Mass.: Addison-Wesley.

Moran, J., and K. Layne. 1988. Enhanced 9-1-1/CAD: interfacing new technology to fight crime. *Police Chief.* 55: 25-29.

Moses, K. 1987. The promise fulfilled: Making local AFIS
    systems work. *Police Chief.* 54: 50-57.

Muchinsky, P. M., and M. L. Tuttle. 1979. Employee
    turnover: An empirical and methodological
    assessment. *Journal of Vocational Behavior.* 14: 43-77.

National Advisory Commission on Criminal Justice Standards
    and Goals. 1973. *Task force on police.* Washington, D.C.:
    U.S. Government Printing Office.

National Center for Prosecution Management. 1974. *Report to the
    Bronx district attorney on the case evaluation system.*
    Washington, D.C.: National Center for Prosecution
    Management.

National Institute of Law Enforcement and Criminal Justice.
    1978. *The national manpower survey of the criminal justice
    system: Vols. 2, 5.* Washington, D.C.: U.S. Government
    Printing Office.

Palumbo, P. A., and G. J. Connor. 1983. Firearms training: The
    computer assisted target analysis system. *Police Chief.*
    50: 67-70.

Pogoloff, K. 1988. Computers animate training. *Law Enforcement
    Technology.* 15: 52-56.

Porter, L. W., and R. M. Steers. 1973. Organizational, work, and
    personal factors in employee turnover and absenteeism.
    Psychological Bulletin. 80: 151-176.

President's Commission on Law Enforcement and
    Administration of Justice. 1967a. *Task force report: The
    police.* Washington, D.C.: U.S. Government Printing
    Office.

President's Commission on Law Enforcement and
    Administration of Justice. 1967b. *Task force report: Science
    and technology.* Washington, D.C.: Government Printing
    Office.

Price, J. L. 1977. *The study of turnover.* Ames, IA: Iowa State.

Ratledge, E. C. 1988. Designing an intelligent computer-aided dispatch system for Delaware State Police. University of Delaware, College of Urban Affairs and Public Policy.

Reboussin, R. 1988. An expert system designed to profile murderers. Paper presented to the Fortieth Annual Meeting of the American Society of Criminology Conference, 9-12 November, Chicago.

Reiss, A. 1971. *The police and the public.* New Haven: Yale.

Rozenberg, J. 1987. *The case for the crown.* Wellingborough, Great Britain: Equation.

Saari, D. 1982. *American court management.* Westport, Conn.: Quorum.

Schrage, M. 1986. "Big Floyd" all wired up to aid G-men. *Washington Post,* 20 July 1.

Shortliffe, E. H. 1976. *Computer-based medical consultations: MYCIN.* New York: Elsevier.

Smith, D. L. 1988. Implementing real world expert systems. *AI Expert.* 3: 51-57.

Smith, N. 1986. Black Hawk County gains by sharing. *Police Chief.* 53: 34.

Smith, P. M. 1988. In-service training for law enforcement personnel. *Law Enforcement Bulletin.* 57: 20-22.

Stone, B. S. 1988. The high-tech beat in St. Pete. *Police Chief.* 55: 23-24.

Tafoya, W. L. 1987. Artificial intelligence. Paper presented to the Eleventh Annual Law Enforcement Information Systems Symposium, Gaithersburg, Maryland. 19-21 August 1-15.

Tien, J. M., J. W. Simon, and R. C. Larson. 1978. *An alternative approach in police patrol: The Wilmington split force experiment.* Washington, D.C.: U.S Government Printing Office.

U.S. Congress. Office of Technology Assessment. 1986.
        Electronic record systems and individual privacy.
        Washington, D.C.: Federal Government
        Information Technology.

Vera Institute of Justice. 1977. *Felony arrests: Their
        prosecution and disposition in New York City's courts.*
        New York: Vera Institute.

Waldron, J., B. Archambeault, W. Archambeault, L. Carsone,
        J. Conser, and C. Sutton. 1987. *Microcomputers in criminal
        justice: Current issues and applications.* Cincinnati:
        Andersen.

Walker, R., and C. J. Flammang. 1980. Law enforcement
        training entering the 1980s. *Police Chief.* 47: 60-64.

Walker, R. O., and C. J. Flammang. 1981. Instructional
        application of computer-based education in police
        training. *Journal of Police Science and Administration.*
        9: 224-228.

Waterman, D. A. 1986. *A guide to expert systems.* Reading,
        Mass.: Addison-Wesley.

Whitaker, G. P., S. Mastrofski, E. Ostrom, R. Parks, and S. L.
        Percey. 1982. *Basic issues in police performance.*
        Washington, D.C.: National Institute of Justice.

Wilkenson, T., and J. Chattin-McNichols. 1985. The
        effectiveness of computer-assisted instruction for
        police officers. *Journal of Police Science and
        Administration.* 13: 230-235.

Wilson, J. Q. 1971. *Varieties of police behavior.* New York:
        Atheneum.

Wilson, T. F., and P. L. Woodard. 1987. *Automated fingerprint
        identification systems: Technology and policy issues.*
        Washington, D.C.: Bureau of Justice Assistance.

INDEX

911 systems 17, 40, 41, 42, 44, 45
Advantages of expert systems 13
    to solve crimes 50
AFIS 24, 25, 30
AID 113, 114
AQ11 114
Arson Information Management
    System (AIMS) 26
Artificial intelligence (AI) 1
    scope 83
    languages 101
Automated fingerprint identification
    systems 24
Automatic interaction detection (AID)
    113
AVM 40

Backward chaining 105, 116
Bayesian probabilities 72
BCPD Expert System
    access for multiple users 128
    costs and program implications
        125
    integration with other detective
        tools 128
    project work steps 119
BCPD expert system for residential
    burglaries 26, 27, 37, 58
BCPD's development costs 36
Big Floyd 1, 2

Building a database of suspects 126
Building the delivery system 73
Building the knowledge base 68
Bureau of Justice Assistance (BJA) 5,
    9, 10, 27
Byrd, Donald 124, 125

C 102, 104, 107, 116
CAI 32, 33, 35
Career criminal-repeat offender
    application 60
    expert system 43, 58, 61, 67, 75
    program 36, 60, 75
CBT 32
Certainty factors 68, 72, 77, 78, 109,
    111, 112
Chaining
    backward 98, 99
    forward 98
COBOL 74, 102
    Command and control 16-22, 39-46
Computer vision 85
Computer-aided dispatch (CAD) 4, 8,
    17, 20, 21, 40, 43, 44, 51, 54, 59,
    62, 110
    Delaware 58, 61
Computer-based training 15, 35
Concept development 62
Conceptual model of
    a burglary 63

a career criminal consultant 66
a dispatcher 65
Conventional languages 107
Coventry Polytechnic 126
Crime-solving 6, 16, 22-24, 32, 61, 76

Decision-making
    real-time, operational 42
    strategic 42
    tactical 42
Detective's assistant 28
Devon and Cornwall Constabulary
        (D&CC) 5, 27, 118-120, 124,
        126
DNA 25-26
    fingerprinting 16
    matching 24, 25
Domain expert 62, 63

Expert systems
    as legal advisers 53
    definition 1
    difficulties 78
    features 3
    law enforcement interest 3
    organizational implications of 13
    role 22, 43
    shell 74, 78
    uses 1, 2
    value of 11, 60

FBI's Violent Criminal Apprehension
        Program 26
Federal Bureau of Investigation (FBI)
        2, 27, 47
FORTRAN 74, 102
Forward chaining 105, 110
Frames 74, 95, 104, 116
    child of the person 95
    instantiation 95
Fuzzy logic 72

Gold Works 115
Government data systems 7

Hardware considerations
    platforms 73
Hardester, Robert 120
Hulbert, John 27
Hyper-text 54

Implementation 73
    strategy(ies) 57, 58
Induction 69
    techniques 114
Inference engine 74-76, 98, 104, 106-
        108, 115-116
Inferencing 77
Information for decision making and
        action 18
Instantiation(s) 105-106
Interview process 68

Jefferson Institute for Justice Studies
        5, 10, 118-120, 122

Knowledge acquisition 57, 62-70, 109,
        111-115
Knowledge base 20-22, 48, 56-57, 60,
        62, 68, 70, 72-75, 77-78, 84, 104,
        107, 108, 115
Knowledge engineer 58, 62-63, 68-70,
        73, 78, 111
    Role of 63
Knowledge engineering 57, 111
Knowledge representation 60, 74, 94,
        104-106, 115-116

Legal training 33-35, 39
    and case attrition 33
    of police 51
LISP 74-75, 101-108
    shell 37
Logic 95
    predicate 97
    propositional 95
Lucas, Robert 118, 126

Magladry, Bruce 120
M.O. 26, 48

matching systems 24, 48
Machine learning 86, 102
Man-machine interaction 69
Managing criminal investigations
    (MCI) 24, 47
MDC 40
Meta-knowledge 100
Meta-rules 73
Miranda 35
Morgan, J. Brian 27
MYCIN 1, 83

National Center for the Analysis of
    Violent Crime (NCAVC) 26
National Institute of Justice 5, 25, 27,
    118, 125
Natural languages 84
New approach with expert systems 20

Operators
    IMPLIES 96
OPS5 106, 107, 108

Pascal 74
PATRIC 26
Personnel management 15, 16, 39
PLATO 32
President's Commission on Law
    Enforcement and
    Administration of Justice 17,
    34
Problem identification 57, 58
Problem size 59
Problem solving 1, 87
Production rule systems problems 100
Production rules 60, 72, 74, 94, 98
Profiling 3, 4, 28, 29
Program planning and design 10
PROLOG 74, 102, 104, 105, 107, 116
PROMIS 13

Ratledge, Edward 4, 119, 120, 123, 127,
    129
Real-time decision-making 4, 20
Reasoning

backward 89
forward 89
Reflections and insights about BCPD
    expert system 126
Relational database(s) 109, 110
Residential burglary(ies) 7, 8, 62, 70
Residential burglary expert system
    30, 37, 39, 51, 60, 61, 65, 77
Robotics 85
Rule based 60
    systems 94, 110

San Bernardino County Sheriff's
    Training Center 35
Savant Research Centre 118, 126
Scripts 97
Search 88
    bi-directional 89
    method(s) 57, 88
    operators 88, 89
    space 88
    strategies 90
        best-first 93
        breadth-first 90
        depth-first 90, 99
        heuristic 93
Selection 108
Semantic networks 97
Shells 37, 75-76, 101, 106, 114-116
Software considerations 74
Solving crimes
    An old story 46
    The case against residential
        burglaries 46
Some new hope in crime-solving 48
Strategic planning 43
Strategies
    inference engine
        control 100
        rule firing 99
Successive differentiation 69
System integration considerations 76

Tactical
    decision-makers 42

deployment 43
Terry v. Ohio 29
The National Advisory Commission
     on Criminal Justice Standards
     and Goals 32
Time dimensions of command and
     control 41
    real-time, operational decision-
      making 42
    strategic decision-making 42
    tactical decision-making 42
Tools 115
Training 9
    academies 53
    courses for investigators 54
    of police 42
    of personnel 31
    programs 32, 33, 35, 52

Uncertainty 24, 25, 43, 58, 60, 72
Uniform and consistent decision
     making 19
Uniform crime reports 46, 47
University of Delaware 119
User interface 74, 79, 115, 116
Users 62
Utilizing organizational databases 109

Validate the knowledge base 70
Validation
    and modification 57, 58, 62, 77
Vera Institute 34
VICAP 26
VP-expert 27

Webb, David W.B. 27

XCON 83

About the Authors

EDWARD C. RATLEDGE is Director of Urban Policy Research at the College of Urban Affairs and Public Policy, Newark, Delaware. Involved in systems design (software engineering and data base design) for 20 years, his expertise ranges from micro-base systems to high end, large scale main frames leading to applications in the fields of criminal justice, natural and human resources, and geographic information systems. He has been widely published in econometric journals as well as applied research journals. They include: *American Economic Review, Review of Economics and Statistics, Advances in Alcohol and Substance Abuse,* and the *Journal of Systems Management,* among others.

JOAN E. JACOBY is Executive Director of the Jefferson Institute for Justice Studies, Washington, D.C. She is the author of *The American Prosecutor: A Search for Identity,* and has contributed chapters to other books including: *Theory and Research in Criminal Justice: Current Perspectives, Preventing Crime, The Prosecutor,* and *The Coming of Age of Information Technology.* Specializing in criminal justice systems and procedures for the past 20 years, she has also authored or co-authored numerous reports including: *Caseweighting Systems for Prosecutors, Basic Issues in Prosecution and Public Defender Performance,* and *Prosecutorial Decisionmaking;* and has been published in the *Journal of Criminal Law and Criminology.*